Microsoft® Office Word 2007

Level 2 (Second Edition)

Microsoft® Office Word 2007: Level 2 (Second Edition)

Part Number: 084894
Course Edition: 1.10

NOTICES

What is the Microsoft Business Certification Program?

The Microsoft Business Certification Program enables candidates to show that they have something exceptional to offer – proven expertise in Microsoft Office programs. The two certification tracks allow candidates to choose how they want to exhibit their skills, either through validating skills within a specific Microsoft product or taking their knowledge to the next level and combining Microsoft programs to show that they can apply multiple skill sets to complete more complex office tasks. Recognized by businesses and schools around the world, over 3 million certifications have been obtained in over 100 different countries. The Microsoft Business Certification Program is the only Microsoft-approved certification program of its kind.

What is the Microsoft Certified Application Specialist Certification?

HELP US IMPROVE OUR COURSEWARE

Your comments are important to us. Please contact us at Element K Press LLC, 1-800-478-7788, 500 Canal View Boulevard, Rochester, NY 14623, Attention: Product Planning, or through our Web site at **http://support.elementkcourseware.com**.

The Microsoft Certified Application Specialist Certification exams focus on validating specific skill sets within each of the Microsoft® Office system programs. The candidate can choose which exam(s) they want to take according to which skills they want to validate. The available Application Specialist exams include:

- Using Microsoft® Windows Vista™
- Using Microsoft® Office Word 2007
- Using Microsoft® Office Excel® 2007
- Using Microsoft® Office PowerPoint® 2007
- Using Microsoft® Office Access 2007
- Using Microsoft® Office Outlook® 2007

What is the Microsoft Certified Application Professional Certification?

The Microsoft Certified Application Professional Certification exams focus on a candidate's ability to use the 2007 Microsoft® Office system to accomplish industry-agnostic functions, for example Budget Analysis and Forecasting, or Content Management and Collaboration. The available Application Professional exams currently include:

- Organizational Support
- Creating and Managing Presentations
- Content Management and Collaboration
- Budget Analysis and Forecasting

What do the Microsoft Business Certification Vendor of Approved Courseware logos represent?

The logos validate that the courseware has been approved by the Microsoft® Business Certification Vendor program and that these courses cover objectives that will be included in the relevant exam. It also means that after utilizing this courseware, you may be prepared to pass the exams required to become a Microsoft Certified Application Specialist or Microsoft Certified Application Professional.

For more information:

To learn more about Microsoft Certified Application Specialist or Professional exams, visit **www.microsoft.com/learning/msbc**.

To learn about other Microsoft Certified Application Specialist approved courseware from Element K, visit **www.elementkcourseware.com**.

* The availability of Microsoft Certified Application exams varies by Microsoft Office program, program version and language. Visit **www.microsoft.com/learning** for exam availability.

Microsoft, the Office Logo, Outlook, and PowerPoint are either registered trademarks or trademarks of Microsoft Corporation in the United States and/or other countries. The Microsoft Certified Application Specialist and Microsoft Certified Application Professional Logos are used under license from Microsoft Corporation.

Microsoft® Office Word 2007: Level 2 (Second Edition)

About This Course

In the first course in this series, *Microsoft® Office Word 2007: Level 1*, you gained all the basic skills that you need to create a wide range of standardized business documents. If you use Microsoft Word 2007 on a regular basis, then once you have mastered the basic skills, the next step is to improve your proficiency. To do so, you can customize and automate the way Microsoft Word 2007 works for you. You can also improve the quality of your work by enhancing your documents with customized Microsoft Word 2007 elements. In this course, you will create complex documents in Microsoft Word 2007 by adding components such as, customized lists, tables, charts, and graphics. You will also create personalized Microsoft Word 2007 efficiency tools.

This course will help you go beyond the basics of word processing to enhance your Microsoft® Office Word 2007 documents with sophisticated components such as tables, charts, customized formats, and graphics. It will also help you create your own Microsoft Word 2007 efficiency tools to produce attractive and effective documents with less time and effort than you've ever needed before.

If your book did not come with a CD, please go to http://www.elementk.com/courseware-file-downloads to download the data files.

This course can also benefit you if you are preparing to take the Microsoft Certified Application Specialist exam for Microsoft® Word 2007. Please refer to the CD-ROM that came with this course for a document that maps exam objectives to the content in the Microsoft Office Word Courseware series. To access the mapping document, insert the CD-ROM into your CD-ROM drive and at the root of the ROM, double-click ExamMapping.doc to open the mapping document. In addition to the mapping document, two assessment files per course can be found on the CD-ROM to check your knowledge. To access the assessments, at the root of the course part number folder, double-click 084894s3.doc to view the assessments without the answers marked, or double-click 084894ie.doc to view the assessments with the answers marked.

Course Description

Target Student

This course was designed for persons who can create and modify standard business documents in Microsoft Word 2007, and who need to learn how to use Microsoft Word 2007 to create or modify complex business documents as well as customized Word efficiency tools. It will be helpful for persons preparing for the Microsoft Certified Application Specialist exams for Microsoft Word 2007.

Course Prerequisites

Students should be able to use Microsoft Word 2007 to create, edit, format, save, and print basic business documents that contain text, basic tables, and simple graphics. Students can obtain this level of skill by taking the following Element K course:

■ *Microsoft® Office Word 2007: Level 1*

How to Use This Book

As a Learning Guide

Each lesson covers one broad topic or set of related topics. Lessons are arranged in order of increasing proficiency with *Microsoft® Office Word 2007*; skills you acquire in one lesson are used and developed in subsequent lessons. For this reason, you should work through the lessons in sequence.

We organized each lesson into results-oriented topics. Topics include all the relevant and supporting information you need to master *Microsoft® Office Word 2007*, and activities allow you to apply this information to practical hands-on examples.

You get to try out each new skill on a specially prepared sample file. This saves you typing time and allows you to concentrate on the skill at hand. Through the use of sample files, hands-on activities, illustrations that give you feedback at crucial steps, and supporting background information, this book provides you with the foundation and structure to learn *Microsoft® Office Word 2007* quickly and easily.

As a Review Tool

Any method of instruction is only as effective as the time and effort you are willing to invest in it. In addition, some of the information that you learn in class may not be important to you immediately, but it may become important later on. For this reason, we encourage you to spend some time reviewing the topics and activities after the course. For additional challenge when reviewing activities, try the "What You Do" column before looking at the "How You Do It" column.

As a Reference

The organization and layout of the book make it easy to use as a learning tool and as an after-class reference. You can use this book as a first source for definitions of terms, background information on given topics, and summaries of procedures.

Course Icons

Icon	Description
	A **Caution Note** makes students aware of potential negative consequences of an action, setting, or decision that are not easily known.
	Display Slide provides a prompt to the instructor to display a specific slide. Display Slides are included in the Instructor Guide only.
	An **Instructor Note** is a comment to the instructor regarding delivery, classroom strategy, classroom tools, exceptions, and other special considerations. Instructor Notes are included in the Instructor Guide only.
	Notes Page indicates a page that has been left intentionally blank for students to write on.
	A **Student Note** provides additional information, guidance, or hints about a topic or task.
	A **Version Note** indicates information necessary for a specific version of software.

Certification

This course is designed to help you prepare for the following certification.

Certification Path: Microsoft Certified Application Specialist – Word 2007

This course is one of a series of Element K courseware titles that addresses Microsoft Certified Application Specialist (Microsoft Business Certification) skill sets. The Microsoft Certified Application Specialist program is for individuals who use Microsoft's business desktop software and who seek recognition for their expertise with specific Microsoft products. Certification candidates must pass one or more proficiency exams in order to earn Microsoft Certified Application Specialist certification.

Course Objectives

In this course, you will create complex documents in Microsoft® Office Word 2007 documents and build personalized efficiency tools in Microsoft Word 2007.

You will:

- manage lists.
- customize tables and charts.
- customize formatting with styles and themes.
- modify pictures in a document.
- create customized graphic elements.
- insert content using Quick Parts.
- control text flow.
- use templates to automate document creation.
- perform mail merges.
- use macros to automate common tasks.

Course Requirements

Hardware

For this course, you will need one computer for each student and one for the instructor. Each computer will need the following minimum hardware components:

- A 1 GHz Pentium-class processor or faster.
- A minimum of 256 MB of RAM. 512 MB of RAM is recommended.
- A 10 GB hard disk or larger. You should have at least 1 GB of free hard disk space available for the Office installation.
- A CD-ROM drive.
- A keyboard and mouse or other pointing device.
- A 1024 x 768 resolution monitor is recommended.
- Network cards and cabling for local network access.
- Internet access (contact your local network administrator).
- A printer (optional) or an installed printer driver.
- A projection system to display the instructor's computer screen.

Software

- Microsoft® Office Professional Edition 2007
- Microsoft Office Suite Service Pack 1
- Windows XP Professional with Service Pack 2

This course was developed using the Windows XP operating system; however, the manufacturer's documentation states that it will also run on Vista. If you use Vista, you might notice some slight differences when keying the course.

Class Setup

Initial Class Setup

1. Install Windows XP Professional on an empty partition.

    ■ Leave the Administrator password blank.

    ■ For all other installation parameters, use values that are appropriate for your environment (see your local network administrator for details).

2. On Windows XP Professional, disable the Welcome screen. (This step ensures that students will be able to log on as the Administrator user regardless of what other user accounts exist on the computer.)

    a. Click Start and choose Control Panel→User Accounts.

    b. Click Change The Way Users Log On And Off.

    c. Uncheck Use Welcome Screen.

    d. Click Apply Options.

3. For Windows XP Professional, install Service Pack 2. Use the Service Pack installation defaults.

4. On the computer, click Start and choose Printers And Faxes. Under Printer Tasks, click Add A Printer and follow the prompts.

5. If you do not have a physical printer, pause the printer object in Windows to avoid printer error messages.

6. Run the Internet Connection Wizard to set up the Internet connection appropriately for your environment, if you did not do so during installation.

7. Display known file type extensions.

    a. Open Windows Explorer (right-click Start and then select Explore).

    b. Choose Tools→Folder Options.

    c. On the View tab, in the Advanced Settings list box, uncheck Hide Extensions For Known File Types.

    d. Click Apply, and then click OK.

    e. Close Windows Explorer.

8. Log on to the computer as the Administrator user if you have not already done so.

9. Perform a complete installation of Microsoft Office Professional 2007.

10. In the User Name dialog box, click OK to accept the default user name and initials.

11. In the Microsoft Office 2007 Activation Wizard dialog box, click Next to activate the Office 2007 application.

12. When the activation of Microsoft Office 2007 is complete, click Close to close the Microsoft Office 2007 Activation Wizard dialog box.

13. In the User Name dialog box, click OK.

14. In the Welcome To Microsoft 2007! dialog box, click Finish. You must have an active Internet connection in order to complete this step. Here, you select the Download And Install Updates From Microsoft Update When Available (Recommended) option, so that whenever there is a new update, it gets automatically installed in your system.

15. After the Microsoft Update runs, in the Microsoft Office Word dialog box, click OK.

16. Minimize the Language Bar, if necessary.

If your book did not come with a CD, please go to **http:// www.elementk.com/ courseware-file-downloads** to download the data files.

17. On the course CD-ROM, open the 084_894 folder. Then, open the Data folder. Run the self-extracting file located in it named 084894dd.exe. This will install a folder named 084894Data on your C drive. This folder contains all the data files that you will use to complete this course.

Within each lesson folder, you may find a Solution folder. This folder contains solution files for the lesson's activities and lesson lab, which can be used by students to check their end results.

Customize the Windows Desktop

Customize the Windows desktop to display the My Computer and My Network Places icon on the student and instructor systems:

1. Right-click the Desktop and choose Properties.

2. Select the Desktop tab.

3. Click Customize Desktop.

4. In the Desktop Items dialog box, check My Computer and My Network Places.

5. Click OK and click Apply.

6. Close the Display Properties dialog box.

Before Every Class

1. Log on to the computer as the Administrator user.

2. Delete the existing C:\084894Data folder and extract a fresh copy of the course data files from the CD-ROM provided with the course manual.

3. Re-create Normal.dotm: close Word, delete C:\Documents and Settings\Administrator\ Application Data\Microsoft\Templates\Normal.dotm, and restart Word.

4. Delete C:\Documents and Settings\Administrator\Application Data\Microsoft\ Templates\My Template.dotx.

5. Delete C:\Documents and Settings\Administrator\Application Data\Microsoft\Templates\ Themes\My Theme1.thmx.

6. In the Word Options dialog box, in the Popular category, uncheck Show Developer Tab In The Ribbon.

7. In the Building Blocks Organizer, delete the Burke Masthead building block from the Quick Parts gallery. Exit Word and click Yes to save the changes to Building Blocks.dotx.

8. If you have a printer driver installed and paused rather than printing to a physical printer, clear all documents from the print queue:

   a. Open the Printers or Printers And Faxes window.

   b. Right-click the printer.

   c. Choose Cancel All Documents.

   d. Click Yes and close the window.

List of Additional Files

Printed with each activity is a list of files students open to complete that activity. Many activities also require additional files that students do not open, but are needed to support the file(s) students are working with. These supporting files are included with the student data files on the course CD-ROM or data disk. Do not delete these files.

1 | **Managing Lists**

Lesson Time: 30 minutes

Lesson Objectives:

In this lesson, you will manage lists.

You will:

● Sort a list.

● Renumber a list.

● Customize a list.

Introduction

You have used lists to enhance the readability of your documents. You can customize these lists based on the type of information you have to present. In this lesson, you will manage lists.

Not all your lists will fit into simple, one-level bulleted or numbered formats. The more kinds of lists you create, the more you'll need to enhance lists to create categories within them, show relationships between list items, and customize a list's appearance to create an effective visual impact. Word provides you with features that help you do all of this and more.

TOPIC A
Sort a List

When you create a list from scratch, the items will appear in the order you enter them. Later, you might find that you need to rearrange the items by sorting the list. In this topic, you will sort a list.

Sorting your list helps you rearrange it in a logical order without the need for tedious cutting and pasting. This means you don't have to worry about the order of the items when you enter them. Also, you can display the information in your list in different ways, depending on your requirements.

Sort Types

There are three different sort types you can use to sort the paragraphs in lists in either ascending or descending order.

Sort Type	Sort Rule
Text	Arranges items that begin with punctuation marks first, followed by items beginning with numbers, and then by individual digits (for instance, 36 will sort before 4). Finally, items beginning with letters are sorted, alphabetically.
	• Ascending: Sorts text from A to Z.
	• Descending: Sorts text from Z to A.
Number	Arranges content by numbers present anywhere in a list item. It sorts the numbers by numeric value (for instance, 4 will sort before 36).
	• Ascending: Sorts the numbers from the lowest to the highest.
	• Descending: Sorts the numbers from the highest to the lowest.
Date	Sorts by both time and date in chronological order.
	• Ascending: Sorts the dates from the earliest to the most recent.
	• Descending: Sorts the dates from the most recent to the earliest.

Sort Fields

Definition:

A *sort field* is an individual item in a list paragraph that can be used as a basis for sorting the list. Multiple sort fields in a list paragraph are separated by a standard character called the sort field separator. Word can use tabs, commas, or any character that you specify as the sort field separator. Sort fields enable you to perform multiple-level sorts on a list of items.

Example:

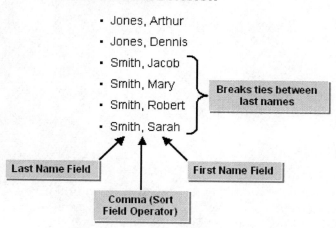

How to Sort a List

Procedure Reference: Sort a List

To sort a list:

1. Select the list or place the insertion point within the list.

2. On the Home tab, in the Paragraph group, click the Sort button to display the Sort Text dialog box.

3. If necessary, specify the sort options.

    a. Click Options to display the Sort Options dialog box.

    b. Specify the sort field separator character in the Separate Fields At section, check the Case Sensitive check box to sort uppercase and lowercase entries separately, and select a sorting language.

    c. Click OK to close the Sort Options dialog box.

4. In the Sort By section, select the primary sort field from the Sort By Using drop-down list, the sort type from the Sort By Type drop-down list, and click Ascending or Descending as the sort order.

5. If necessary, in the Then By section, from the Sort By drop-down list, select the additional fields you want to sort by.

6. If necessary, in the My List Has section, select Header Row or No Header Row to exclude or include the first row of the table in the sort.

7. Click OK to perform the sort.

ACTIVITY 1-1
Sorting a List

Data Files:

Burke List.docx

Before You Begin:

Open Microsoft Word.

Scenario:

You're preparing a memo for Jan Burke, the president of Burke Properties, to inform her of the names of new agents hired in various territories. You've entered the agents' names into a list in the order you received them from the hiring manager. However, you think that the memo would be easier to read if the agents were listed by their last name.

What You Do	How You Do It
1. **Open the Word document.**	a. **Click the Microsoft Office button and choose Open.**
	b. In the Open dialog box, from the Look In drop-down list, **navigate to C:\084894Data\Managing Lists.**
	c. **Select Burke List.docx and click Open.**

2. Sort the list by the agents' last names.

a. In the Burke List document, **scroll down and select all the rows in the bulleted list.**

b. On the Home tab, in the Paragraph group, **click the Sort button.**

c. In the Sort Text dialog box, in the Sort By drop-down list, **verify that the default sort order is to sort text paragraphs in ascending order.**

d. In the My List Has section, **verify that the No Header Row option is selected and click OK** to sort the list by the agents' last names.

e. **Save the file as *My Burke List.docx*.**

ACTIVITY 1-2

Sorting a List by Fields

Setup:

My Burke List.docx is open.

Scenario:

The Human Resources Director has reviewed your memo and recommends that Jan Burke would prefer to see the sales agents' names listed by their territories. You would prefer not to have to retype the list so that the territory names appear first in each list paragraph, so you decide to sort the existing list in a different order.

What You Do	How You Do It
1. Specify the sort field separator to sort on the second field.	a. On the Home tab, in the Paragraph group, **click the Show/Hide button** ¶ to display the non-printing characters.
	b. In the Burke Fields List document, **scroll down** and verify that the agents' names and territories are separated by a tab character.

- → Ansely, Arnold → Baltimore, MD¶
- → Boyer, Bridget → Toledo, OH¶
- → Janowski, Erin → Daytona, Florida¶
- → Valley, Mike → Lexington, KY¶

	c. **Select the complete bulleted list.**
	d. On the Home tab, in the Paragraph group, **click the Sort button.**
	e. In the Sort Text dialog box, **click Options.**

f. In the Sort Options dialog box, in the Separate Fields At section, **verify that the Tabs option is selected by default and click OK.**

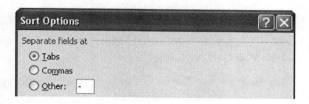

2. **Sort the list by the second field.**

a. In the Sort Text dialog box, from the Sort By drop-down list, **select Field 2.**

b. **Verify that the sort type will be Text, Ascending, and click OK.**

c. The list is sorted by the territories. **Save and close the file.**

TOPIC B
Renumber a List

You have sorted a variety of lists. While numbering lists, you may find that you need to interrupt the list with additional information, or restart numbering within an existing list. In this topic, you will renumber a list.

Sometimes a list has to be stopped and started again, perhaps to insert commentary about one of the items. You may sometimes find that the list you are working on is starting to get too long and it would be a good idea to split the list in two. Renumbering a list lets you handle such situations. You can choose to continue numbering after adding an extra paragraph of information into a list, or you can restart numbering in cases where two lists would work better than one.

Renumbering Options

Renumbering options are useful when you need to include additional information between list items while retaining the numbering sequence. These options also help split a list. The Set Numbering Value dialog box has options to start a new list or continue numbering from the previous list. You can launch this dialog box by clicking the Numbering button drop-down arrow and selecting Set Numbering Value. You can also turn off a list and turn it back on using the Numbering button on the Home tab.

How to Renumber a List

Procedure Reference: Continue a Numbered List

To continue a numbered list:

1. Turn on numbering, and enter the first few items into the list.
2. To turn off numbering, press Enter twice, or press Enter once and click the Numbering button.
3. Enter the paragraphs that do not need numbers.
4. Press Enter to insert a new list item.
5. To turn on numbering for the new list item, on the Home tab, in the Paragraph group, click the Numbering button, or right-click the item and choose Numbering.
6. To continue the numbering from the previous list, right-click the item and choose Continue Numbering.
7. Enter the remaining items in the list.

Procedure Reference: Restart a Numbered List Using the Set Numbering Value Dialog Box

To restart a numbered list using the Set Numbering Value dialog box:

1. Place the insertion point on the item after which a new list should begin.
2. Display the Set Numbering Value dialog box.
   - On the Home tab, in the Paragraph group, from the Numbering button drop-down list, select Set Numbering Value.
   - Or, right-click and choose Set Numbering Value.
3. If necessary, in the Set Numbering Value dialog box, select the Start New List option.

4. In the Set Value To spin box, set the value to 1.
5. Click OK to restart a numbered list and to close the dialog box.

 Right-clicking an item of the list and choosing Restart At 1 starts a new list from that list item.

ACTIVITY 1-3

Renumbering a List

Data Files:

Burke Numbered List.docx

Before You Begin:

From C:\084894Data\Managing Lists, open Burke Numbered List.docx.

Scenario:

You need to create a memo to inform hiring managers of the steps they need to take when hiring new employees. You've created part of the memo, including the first five items in the list. You may need to add additional comments in separate paragraphs for specific list items.

What You Do	How You Do It
1. Add a comment to the last item in the numbered list.	a. In the Burke Numbered List document, **position the insertion point at the end of the last list item in the numbered list and press Enter** to start a new line.
	b. On the Home tab, in the Paragraph group, **click the Numbering button** to turn off numbering.
	c. **Click the Increase Indent button** to align the insertion point with the list items.
	d. **Type *Note: Include an HR orientation session in the agenda.* and press Enter.**
2. Complete the numbered list.	a. On the Home tab, in the Paragraph group, **click the Numbering button** to turn on numbering.
	b. In the Burke Numbered List document, **right-click and choose Continue Numbering.**
	c. **Type *Please greet the new employee at the door on the first day.***
	d. **Save the document as *My Burke Numbered List.docx* and close it.**

TOPIC C
Customize Lists

You created and structured different types of lists. You find that your list still needs some fine-tuning so that it looks more appealing to your audience. In this topic, you will customize the appearance of lists.

Sometimes, you may find that your list needs an option that's just a little bit different from the ones provided. You might need to create a multilevel list, combine bullets and numbers within your list, tighten up the spacing on the list to fit more information on each line, or you might need to call more attention to certain parts of the list. Word allows you to customize lists as you desire.

Multilevel Lists

Definition:

A *multilevel list* is a list with a hierarchical structure. The number or bullet format is configured separately for each level of the list. The list can mix numbers on some levels with bullets on other levels. Items on lower levels of the multilevel list can be demoted, by indenting to the right, to distinguish them from items on higher levels.

Example:

Converting an Existing Numbered List

You can convert items in a numbered list to a multilevel list format simply by demoting entries in the list. Word automatically applies the multilevel list format to the new subordinate step.

List Styles

Definition:

A *list style* is a style that contains list-specific formatting options. List styles can contain the formatting characteristics of both numbered and bulleted lists, and can be applied to one or more levels of a list. A list style has number or bullet formatting for up to nine levels by default. Each level can be individually formatted. Since a list style is a type of style itself, it cannot contain paragraph styles.

Example:

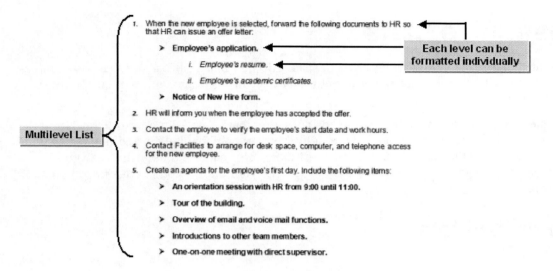

The Multilevel List Gallery

The Multilevel List button in the Paragraph group displays a gallery of predefined list styles that can be directly applied to text. The gallery is split into four sections: the first section displays the list style that is currently chosen, the second section displays predefined list styles, the third section contains the customized list styles, and the last section contains options to modify the list styles.

List Appearance Customization Options

There are a variety of options you can configure to customize the appearance of your list, based on the list type.

Option	Description
Bullet Character	You can set a symbol, picture, or font as the bullet character. The Define New Bullet dialog box has buttons that control the choice of symbol or picture used as the bullet, and the font from which the bullet can be selected.
Bullet Position	You can set the position of the bullet with respect to the page margin. The Alignment section in the Define New Bullet dialog box specifies if the bullet has to be aligned left, center, or to the right of the page margin.
Text Position	You can set the spacing between the bullet and the list item. The Text Indent At spin box in the Define New Multilevel List dialog box controls the amount of space between the bullet or number and the text in the list item.
Number Format	You can also set different number styles or fonts as the number format for a list. The Define New Number Format dialog box controls the style of numbering (Arabic numerals, Roman numerals, letters, and so on) and the font from which the numbers are selected.
Number Position	You can also set the numbering position of the list with respect to the page margin. The Alignment section in the Define New Number Format dialog box specifies if the number has to be aligned left, center, or right.

How to Customize a List

Procedure Reference: Create a New Multilevel List

To create a new multilevel list:

1. On the Home tab, in the Paragraph group, click the Multilevel List button.

2. In the Multilevel List gallery, in the List Library section, select a list style.

3. Enter the list items.

4. Change the level of specific list items.

   a. To demote a list item, select the item and press Tab, or, on the Home tab, in the Paragraph group, click the Increase Indent button.

   b. To promote a list item, select the item and press Shift+Tab, or, on the Home tab, in the Paragraph group, click the Decrease Indent button.

Procedure Reference: Customize List Appearance

To customize list appearance:

1. Select the level of the list that you want to customize.

2. Display the corresponding gallery for the list type.

   - On the Home tab, in the Paragraph group, click the drop-down arrow next to the button that corresponds to the list type.

   - Or, right-click and choose Bullets or Numbering.

3. To convert a portion of the list from numbers to bullets or from bullets to numbers, select the number or bullet style from the gallery.

4. To customize the appearance of a portion of the list, select the list appearance options from the appropriate gallery.

   - To customize bullets, click Define New Bullet.

     - From the Bullet Alignment drop-down list, select left, center, or right.

     - Click Symbol or Picture to use a symbol or picture as the bullet character.

     - Click Font to select and customize the font for the bullet character.

   - To customize numbers, click Define New Number Format.

     - From the Number Style drop-down list, select an existing number style.

     - In the Number Format text box, type your desired number format.

     - From the Number Alignment drop-down list, select left, center, or right.

     - Click Font to select and customize the font for the numbers.

5. When you are done with each gallery, click OK.

ACTIVITY 1-4

Customizing a List

Data Files:

Multilevel Report.docx

Before You Begin:

From C:\084894Data\Managing Lists, open Multilevel Report.docx.

Scenario:

You need to create a draft of the annual stockholder report for your company. You've begun to draft a list of the main points that you will need to cover in the report and you plan to add a few more items before presenting it to the president of the organization. You realize that there is no clear distinction between the main points and sublevel items in the list.

What You Do	How You Do It
1. **Apply a multilevel list format.**	a. In the document, **select all the items listed under Draft Outline.**
	b. On the Home tab, in the Paragraph group, **click the Multilevel List drop-down arrow.**
	c. In the Multilevel List gallery, in the List Library section, **click the first multilevel list style to the right of the None option** to apply it to the list.

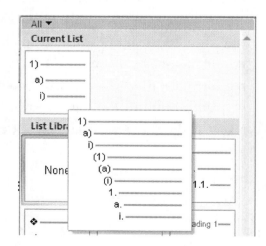

2. **Demote the items below each main point.**

   a. In the document, **position the insertion point at the beginning of the line that states "This year's accomplishments" and press Tab** to demote the list item.

   b. **Position the insertion point at the beginning of the "Next year's goals" list item and press Tab** to demote the list item.

   c. **Demote the last two items of the list.**

3. **Add the managers' names as the sublevel items to "New relocation team".**

   a. In the document, **position the insertion point at the end of "New relocation team", and press Enter** to add a new list item.

   b. **Press Tab** to demote the new list item by one level.

> **▪ *Stockholder·Annual·Report*¶**
>
> **▪ Draft·Outline¶**
>   ¶
>   1)→President's·Message¶
>   a)→This·year's·accomplishments¶
>   b)→Next·year's·goals¶
>   2)→Organizational·Growth¶
>   a)→Departmental·reorganization¶
>   b)→New·relocation·team¶
>   i)→

   c. The new list level starts with a lowercase Roman numeral. **Type *Pat Markus* and press Enter.**

   d. **Type *Daniel Ortiz***

4. **The two new team members should appear in a bullet list to show that neither one has priority. Convert the lowest level of the list to a bullet format.**

   a. **Select the Pat Markus and Daniel Ortiz lines in the list.**

   b. In the Paragraph group, **click the Bullets button** to convert this section of the list to bullets.

5. **Customize the bullet of the lowest level of the list.**

a. In the Paragraph group, **click the Multi-level List drop-down arrow and choose Define New Multilevel List.**

b. In the Define New Multilevel List dialog box, in the Click Level To Modify list box, **verify that 3 is selected.**

c. In the Number Format section, from the Number Style For This Level drop-down list, **scroll down and select the bullet with the right-pointing arrow.**

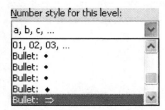

d. **Click OK.**

e. **Click outside the list** to deselect it.

f. **Save the document as *My Burke Multilevel Report.docx* and close it.**

Lesson 1 Follow-up

In this lesson, you customized and managed a variety of lists in Word documents. Because lists are such a common element in documents, knowing how to customize and enhance them will help you organize and present your list information more effectively.

1. **What types of lists have you seen in the business documents you work with? How do you think you can improve the display of these lists?**

2. **Which of Word's list management features are you most likely to use at work? Why?**

2 Customizing Tables and Charts

Lesson Time: 45 minutes

Lesson Objectives:

In this lesson, you will customize tables and charts.

You will:

- Sort table data.
- Control cell layout.
- Perform calculations in a table.
- Create charts to visually represent numerical data.

Introduction

You have managed and customized lists in your documents. Similarly, tables can be customized to enhance the presentation of the data. In addition, you can represent table data as charts in your documents. In this lesson, you will customize tables and charts.

Formatting the structure and appearance of your basic tables can help you create great looking tables. In addition to changing the position of text or the structure of the cells in your table, you can even customize the data in your table by performing calculations on numerical data or sorting your data. Word even lets you support your table information by displaying it as a chart in your document.

TOPIC A
Sort Table Data

In this lesson, you will customize tables and charts that are based on tables. One of the simplest and most common ways that you might customize your table is to sort the data in it. In this topic, you will sort table data.

You may need to organize employee information tabular data in alphabetical order or sales figures in numeric order. Having to cut and paste to move row data is tedious and error prone. Word allows you to quickly sort table data in the way that best suits your needs.

Table Sort Options

You have several options that enable you to control how data is sorted in a table.

- You can use column headings as fields for sorting the data.
- You can include or exclude the header row of the table from the sort.
- You can sort on multiple levels by using field delimiters within column data.

How to Sort a Table

Procedure Reference: Sort a Table

To sort a table:

1. Select the text that needs to be sorted.
    - Select the entire table, including the first row, if this row contains column headings you want to use to identify the sort order.
    - Select only the rows in the table that contain data if you want to sort by fields within one of the table columns.
    - Select an entire column if you want to sort the data in the column by fields.
2. If necessary, in the Sort dialog box, set the sort field separator character, define a case-sensitive sort, or select the sorting language.
3. In the Sort By section, define the sort field, sort type, and sort order.
4. If necessary, in the Then By section, from the Sort By drop-down list, specify the additional fields you want to sort by.
5. If necessary, in the My List Has section, select the No Header row option to exclude the header row from the sort.
6. Click OK to perform the sort.

ACTIVITY 2-1

Sorting Data in a Table

Data Files:

Mortgage Letter.docx

Before You Begin:

From C:\084894Data\Customizing Tables and Charts, open Mortgage Letter.docx.

Scenario:

You're preparing a letter for a real estate client who has inquired about comparative mortgage loan rates. The letter includes a table of loan rates. The first row of the table contains descriptive column headings. After drafting the letter, you realize that the client will probably want the information listed alphabetically by city.

What You Do	How You Do It
1. **Select the loan rates table.**	a. In the Mortgage Letter document, **click in the "Location" cell in the table** to display the Table Tools Layout contextual tab.
	b. On the Table Tools Layout contextual tab, in the Table group, **click Select** and from the displayed drop-down menu, **choose Select Table.**

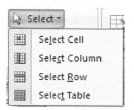

2. Sort the data in the table.

a. In the Data group, **click the Sort button.**

b. In the Sort dialog box, in the Sort By section, from the first drop-down list, **select Location.**

c. **Verify that the sort type is Text using Paragraphs and select Ascending.**

d. In the My List Has section, **verify that the Header Row option is selected by default.** This indicates that the first row will be excluded in the sort.

e. **Click OK** to sort the table.

f. **Save the document as** *My Mortgage Letter.docx* **and close it.**

TOPIC B
Control Cell Layout

In the previous topic, you changed the overall order of the table contents by sorting the table. It is also possible to change the configuration of individual cells in the table. In this topic, you will control cell layout.

Cell layout options such as merging and splitting cells are useful when you want a table that's not a plain grid-like structure. Imagine a table with a title in a single big cell that spans the width of all the other columns, or a cell entry that needs to be broken up into two sections. Controlling cell layout lets you manage the cell shape and placement in these situations.

Cell Layout Options

There are four main ways that you can control the layout of cells.

- Merge cells together.
- Split cells apart.
- Change the text alignment in a cell.
- Change the direction of text in a cell.

Cell Merge

Definition:

Cell merge is a method of altering the configuration of groups of cells in a table. The group of cells to be merged should be placed adjacent to each other in order to form one single, larger cell. The cells that are to be merged together can be from multiple rows or columns. The new cell will be the size and shape of the original selection.

Example:

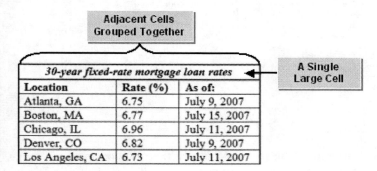

Merging Cells Containing Content

If you merge several cells that contain content, the information in the first cell will appear as the first paragraph in the merged cell, the information in the second cell will appear as the second paragraph in the merged cell, and so on.

Cell Split

Definition:

Cell split is a method of dividing a table cell. The cell split can be performed only on a single cell. The new cells formed take up the same amount of space as the original cells. Cell split can result in the division of a cell into two or more adjacent cells.

Example:

Project Code Name	Project Manager
Atlas	Jim Simpson
Midas	Judy Rodriguez
Cassandra	Marilyn Beck (Phase 1)
	Jim Simpson (Phase 2)

Cell split resulting in two adjacent cells

Splitting Multiple Cells

You can also split multiple cells. When you do this, you have the option to merge the cells first before splitting them into a different arrangement.

Cell Alignment

Definition:

Cell alignment is a text-positioning option that enables you to control the placement of text within one or more cells. The nine cell-alignment options enable you to align cell contents vertically to the top, center, or bottom of the cell, and horizontally to the left, center, or right of the cell.

Example:

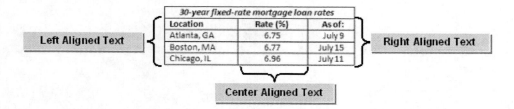

Left Aligned Text

30-year fixed-rate mortgage loan rates		
Location	Rate (%)	As of:
Atlanta, GA	6.75	July 9
Boston, MA	6.77	July 15
Chicago, IL	6.96	July 11

Right Aligned Text

Center Aligned Text

Text Direction

Definition:

Text direction is a text-positioning option that enables you to change the orientation of the text flow. You can change the direction of text to display text either horizontally, vertically upward, or vertically downward. Text direction options can be set for text within a cell, a text box, or a shape. In cell text direction, the height of the cells will change automatically to accommodate vertical direction, but this is not the case in shapes and text boxes.

Example:

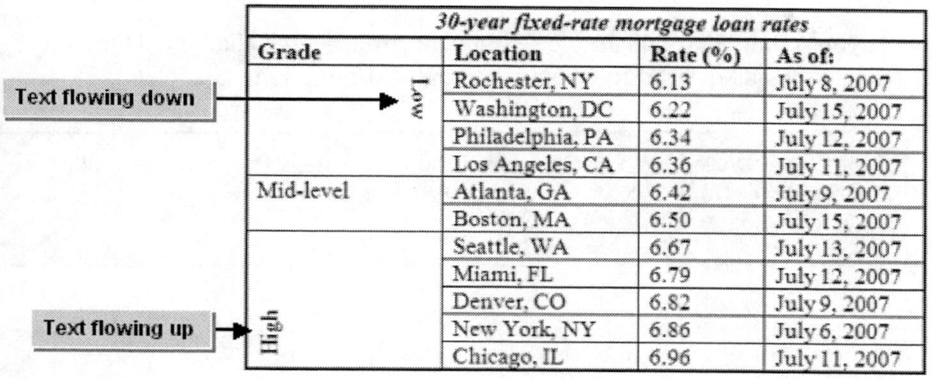
Text flowing down
Text flowing up

30-year fixed-rate mortgage loan rates			
Grade	Location	Rate (%)	As of:
Low	Rochester, NY	6.13	July 8, 2007
	Washington, DC	6.22	July 15, 2007
	Philadelphia, PA	6.34	July 12, 2007
	Los Angeles, CA	6.36	July 11, 2007
Mid-level	Atlanta, GA	6.42	July 9, 2007
	Boston, MA	6.50	July 15, 2007
High	Seattle, WA	6.67	July 13, 2007
	Miami, FL	6.79	July 12, 2007
	Denver, CO	6.82	July 9, 2007
	New York, NY	6.86	July 6, 2007
	Chicago, IL	6.96	July 11, 2007

How to Control Cell Layout

Procedure Reference: Merge or Split Cells

To merge or split cells:

1. Select the cells that you want to restructure.
   - Select adjacent cells to perform a cell merge.
   - Place the insertion point in the cell you want to split to perform a cell split.
2. Modify the structure of the cells, as required.
   - Merge the cells.
     - On the Layout contextual tab, in the Merge group, click the Merge Cells button.
     - Or, right-click the selected cells and choose Merge Cells.
   - Split a cell.
     a. Display the Split Cells dialog box.
        - On the Layout contextual tab, in the Merge group, click the Split Cells button.
        - Or, right-click the selected cells and choose Split Cells.

     b. In the Split Cells dialog box, type the number of columns and rows you want to split the cell into.

     c. Click OK to close the dialog box.

Procedure Reference: Change the Alignment or Direction of Text in Cells

To change the alignment or direction of text in cells:

1. Select the cells.
2. Specify the alignment.
   - Right-click the selection, choose Cell Alignment, and select the desired alignment.
   - Or, on the Table Tools Layout contextual tab, in the Alignment group, select the desired alignment.
3. Specify the text direction.
   - Specify the text direction using the Text Direction - Table Cell dialog box.
     a. Right-click the selected cells and choose Text Direction.

b.   In the Text Direction - Table Cell dialog box, select the desired direction.

c.   Click OK.

● Or, on the Layout contextual tab, in the Alignment group, click the Text Direction button as many times as desired to select the preferred direction.

Each time you click the Text Direction button, the orientation of the text changes. The direction of the icon also changes according to the changing direction of the text.

ACTIVITY 2-2

Controlling Cell Layout

Data Files:

Modified Mortgage Letter.docx

Before You Begin:

From C:\084894Data\Customizing Tables and Charts, open Modified Mortgage Letter.docx.

Scenario:

Looking at your mortgage rates table, you realize that you could use your introductory paragraph as a title row within the table. However, the text is too long to fit in a single table cell at the current cell width. You also want to update information on a city that has the same mortgage rates as Los Angeles, California. You want to emphasize that the mortgages are graded high, medium, and low, and also want to ensure that the top row of the table doesn't blend with the other table content.

What You Do	How You Do It
1. **Insert a new title row.**	a. In the Modified Mortgage Letter document, **click in the first cell after the text "Grade"** to position the insertion point in the first row in the table.
	b. On the Table Tools Layout contextual tab, in the Rows & Columns group, **click Insert Above** to insert the new row.
2. **Merge the cells in the new title row.**	a. **Verify that all the cells in the new row are selected.**
	b. On the Layout contextual tab, in the Merge group, **click the Merge Cells button.**

3. **Move the text into the new title row.**

   a. Select the text **"30-year fixed-rate mortgage loan rates"** that appears above the table.

   b. On the Home tab, in the Clipboard group, **click the Cut button.**

   c. **Click in the newly inserted title row in the table.**

   d. On the Home tab, in the Clipboard group, **click the Paste button.**

> You can also drag the selected text into the cell to move it.

4. **Center the text in the title row.**

   a. **Place the insertion point in the title row of the table before "30-year".**

   b. On the Table Tools Layout contextual tab, in the Alignment group, **click the Align Center button** to center the text in the cell.

30-year fixed-rate mortgage loan rates			
Grade	**Location**	**Rate (%)**	**As of:**
—	Rochester NY	6.13	July 8, 2007

5. **Split a cell and insert new text in the cell.**

a. **Click in the cell with the text "Los Angeles, CA".**

b. On the Table Tools Layout contextual tab, in the Merge group, **click Split Cells.**

c. In the Split Cells dialog box, in the Number of Columns text box, **type *1***

d. In the Number Of Rows text box, **type *2***

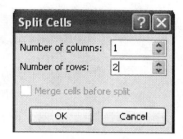

e. **Click OK** to split the cell into two rows.

f. **Click in the new empty cell and type *San Diego, CA***

6. **Align the text to the right of the newly split cells.**

a. **Select the two cells to the right of the newly split cells.**

b. In the Alignment group, **click the Align Center Left button.**

7. **Change the direction of text in two of the cells.**

a. In the 30-Year Fixed-Rate Mortgage Loan Rates table, **place the insertion point in the first cell in the third row just before "Low".**

b. On the Table Tools Layout contextual tab, in the Alignment group, **click Text Direction** to change the text flow vertically downward.

c. **Place the insertion point in the last cell of the first column just before the text "High".**

d. **Click Text Direction twice** to change the text flow vertically upward.

High	Seattle, WA	6.67	July 13, 2007
	Miami, FL	6.79	July 12, 2007
	Denver, CO	6.82	July 9, 2007
	New York, NY	6.86	July 6, 2007
	Chicago, IL	6.96	July 11, 2007

e. **Save the document as** *My Modified Mortgage Letter.docx* **and close it.**

TOPIC C
Perform Calculations in a Table

So far in this lesson, you've managed the appearance or layout of the table. Another way you can customize tables is to perform simple calculations on numeric information in the tables. In this topic, you'll perform calculations in a table.

Word processing is mostly about words, but once you start putting numbers in tables, it starts to be about math, too. You can't get the most out of your numbers without applying calculations to them. Whether the calculations are totals, averages, or simple addition and subtraction, you can use them in your tables to help you generate values without having to manually calculate and enter them yourself.

Formulas in Word

Definition:

A *formula* is a mathematical expression that can be used to perform calculations on data in a Word document. A formula starts with an equal sign, which is followed either by a function and arguments, or by mathematical constants and operators. In Word, the results of the formula do not update when the numbers the formula is based on change; you must manually update the results of the formula.

 Word formulas are intended for simple, one-time calculations on small groups of numbers, often in a table. If you need to perform more complex calculations, you should use a dedicated spreadsheet application, such as Microsoft® Office Excel® 2007.

Example:

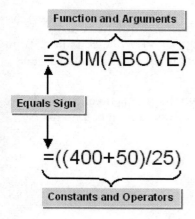

Function and Arguments

=SUM(ABOVE)

Equals Sign

=((400+50)/25)

Constants and Operators

Functions

Definition:

A *function* is a predefined expression that performs an operation on a set of values called *arguments*. Each function has a unique name followed by a set of parentheses within which the arguments can be specified. Each function can perform different operations on the provided arguments. A function can take either numbers, cell references, or names that describe the position of the cells. The arguments in a function are separated by commas.

Example:

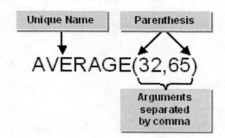

Common Functions in Word

There are a variety of predefined functions that can be used to perform simple calculations on data within a table. The SUM function performs addition on the provided arguments. SUM is commonly used in tables to create totals. For example, the function SUM(100,200) would display the value 300 in a table cell. Besides the SUM function, other common functions include AVERAGE, which returns an average of the arguments, and PRODUCT, which multiplies the arguments.

Arguments

Arguments are enclosed in parentheses after the function name and separated by commas. You can include any of the following as valid arguments in a function:

- Numbers.

- Names of adjacent groups of cells: The name describes the position of the cells in relation to the formula cell. For example, the (LEFT) argument refers to all the cells that contain numbers that are to the left of the formula cell.

- Table references: Table references assign a grid letter and number to each cell in the table. The columns are assigned letters from left to right, and the rows are assigned numbers from top to bottom.

Equations

Definition:

An *equation* in Microsoft Word is a specialized document element that can contain complex mathematical symbols and perform customized calculations. An equation can contain numbers and letters, but can also contain specialized mathematical symbols and operators not normally available in the basic document font. The components of the equation can be aligned, oriented, or sized in any way necessary to form the desired mathematical expression. To insert equations into tables or other text within Word documents, you can use the *Equation Tool,* a contextual feature built into Word 2007. You can insert standard equation types and then edit them, or you can build new equations.

 For more information on equations and the Equation Tool, see the Microsoft Word online Help system.

Example:

Mathematical Symbols

$$(x + a)^n = \sum_{k=0}^{n} \binom{n}{k} x^k a^{n-k}$$

Components aligned to form expression

How to Perform Calculations in a Table

Procedure Reference: Insert Formulas in a Table

To insert formulas in a table:

1. Place the insertion point in the cell where you want to put the formula result.
2. On the Table Tools Layout contextual tab, in the Data group, click the Formula button to open the Formula dialog box.
3. Type the formula in the Formula text box, or select the appropriate function from the Paste Function drop-down list.
4. If necessary, from the Number Format drop-down list, select the desired number format. By default, the format of the calculation result will match the format of the numbers used in the calculation.
5. Click OK to insert the formula into the table.
6. If necessary, repeat the formula you inserted last by pressing F4.
7. If you change data in the table, select the cell with the formula and press F9 to update the formula results.

Displaying Field Codes and Field Results

Word inserts formulas into documents as fields. If you prefer to see the field codes for the formula itself in a table cell, rather than the formula result, you can right-click the formula cell and choose Toggle Field Codes. Toggle the codes again to switch back to the result. To switch between field codes and field results globally in the Word application, you can press Alt+F9, or you can open the Word Options dialog box, select the Advanced tab and, in the Show Document Content section, check or uncheck Show Field Codes Instead Of Their Values.

Default Formula Entries

When you display the Formula dialog box, the Formula text box will typically default to =SUM(ABOVE) if there are any numbers in the cells above the formula cell. If there are no numbers in the cells above the formula cell, the formula will default to =SUM(LEFT). To insert a different formula, delete the =SUM function from the Formula text box.

ACTIVITY 2-3

Performing Calculations in a Table

Data Files:

Loan Rates.docx

Before You Begin:

From C:\084894Data\Customizing Tables and Charts, open Loan Rates.docx.

Scenario:

You are creating an information sheet for customers to illustrate how affordable home improvement loans can be. You've created a table showing all the various loan cost figures; the only detail missing is the totals. Also, the totals need to be in the currency format.

What You Do	How You Do It
1. **Insert formulas to calculate the totals for the first three columns of the table.**	a. In the Loan Rates document, in the table, **place the insertion point in the empty cell at the bottom of the First Year column.**
	b. On the Table Tools Layout contextual tab, in the Data group, **click the Formula button** to display the Formula dialog box.
	c. In the Formula text box, **verify that the =SUM(ABOVE) formula is displayed and click OK** to insert the formula into the table cell.

	First Year
Principal	$2,457.09
Interest	$551.20
Annual Totals	$3,008.29

d. **Use =SUM(ABOVE) to add the totals to the bottom of the Second Year and Third Year columns.**

2. **Insert formulas to calculate the totals for the last column of the table.**

a. In the Principal row, **place the insertion point in the first empty cell of the Total column.**

b. **Display the Formula dialog box.**

c. In the Formula text box, **verify that the formula reads =SUM(LEFT) and click OK** to insert the formula into the table cell.

d. **Place the insertion point in the empty cell at the end of the Interest row.**

e. **Display the Formula dialog box,** and in the Formula text box, **modify the formula to read =SUM(LEFT).**

f. From the Number Format drop-down list, **select the third number format and click OK** to include a comma and dollar sign in the formula result.

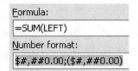

g. **Place the insertion point in the empty cell at the end of the Annual Totals row.**

h. **Press F4** to repeat the calculation and calculate the grand total of the cost over the life of the loan.

i. **Save the document as *My Loan Rates.docx* and close it.**

TOPIC D
Create Charts

You have worked with tables containing numeric information. Another way to display numeric information is to transfer it to a chart. In this topic, you will create charts to visually represent numerical data.

A picture is worth a thousand words, and a chart is worth a table full of numbers. Charts can help the people reading your document better understand the relationships between the figures presented in the table.

Charts

Definition:

A *chart* is a visual representation of data from a table or worksheet that is used to present complex and numerical information symbolically. Each column or other symbol in the chart represents the value of one item of data. A chart contains items such as axes, data values, legends, labels and titles. There is a variety of chart types, such as column charts, line graphs, or pie charts.

Example:

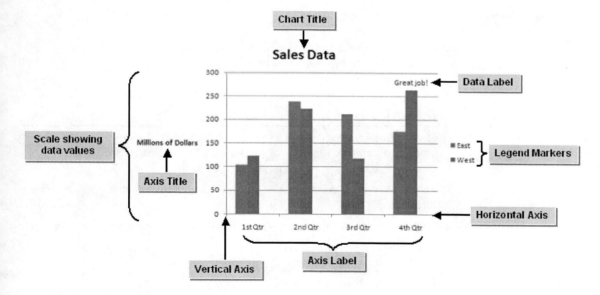

Chart Components

Charts can have a number of specialized components.

Chart Component	Description
Horizontal, Vertical, and Depth axes	An axis is the line that depicts values against which the chart data is plotted. Depending on the chart type, the horizontal axis (x-axis) appears at the bottom of the chart; the vertical axis (y-axis) is plotted at 90 degrees to the horizontal axis. 3-D charts have a depth axis (z-axis). Pie charts have only one axis, which wraps around the chart.
Scale	The range of values on the axis. It is derived from the values in the original table.
Legend	A visual indicator of which sections of the chart relate to which sets of values in the table. It is derived from text in the original table.
Chart title	Descriptive text added to the chart as a whole.
Axis labels	Descriptions of the data plotted against an axis.
Data labels	Descriptive text added to individual values in the chart.

Chart Types

There are several categories of chart types, each of which is designed to suit a particular type of data or to represent a specific relationship between numbers.

Chart Type	Depicts
Column or Bar	Comparisons among categories of items. The stacked subtypes of the column charts portray relations of parts to a whole. A bar chart is a column chart with the x-axis on the left instead of at the bottom of the chart.
Line or Area	Trends over time. An area chart is a line chart with the area under the line filled in.
Pie	Relations of parts to a whole. A pie chart shows a single set of numbers in a circle.
Doughnut	Relations between data sets in concentric circles.
X Y (Scatter)	Relations between pairs of values.
Stock	High-low-close-open values for commodities traded in a market or exchange.
Surface	Trends resulting from the combinations of two sets of data. A surface chart is used to find the optimum combination of values for two variables.
Bubble	Relations among three variables. Essentially, it is an XYZ-type scatter chart; the size of the bubble represents the value of the third variable.
Radar	Comparisons between aggregate values in multiple sets of numbers.

The Chart In Microsoft Office Word Window

The Chart In Microsoft Office Word window is a supplemental application that provides the charting functions to Word and the other Microsoft Office applications. You must use this tool to enter the data on which your charts are based. Whenever you create or modify a chart, Word automatically activates the Microsoft Excel functions in a separate interface. The Excel sheet has default data for a chart; and you can edit the default data or paste in data from a table in a Word document.

Chart Tools

When you select a chart that is inserted into a Word document, the Chart Tools contextual tab appears with three tabs that help in formatting and structuring the chart.

Contextual Tab	Function
Design	Provides options to edit the chart type, data, chart layout, and styles.
Layout	Provides options to add shapes, titles, labels, change the background, and analyze chart trends.
Format	Provides options to format elements within the chart and arrange text in the chart.

How to Create a Chart

Procedure Reference: Create a Chart

To create a chart:

1. On the Insert tab, in the Illustrations group, click the Chart button.

2. In the Insert Chart dialog box, in the right pane, select a chart type.

3. If necessary, in the left pane, select a chart subtype and click OK.

4. In the Excel worksheet that is displayed, delete the generic data and enter new data, or paste in data from the table you want to use as the basis for the chart.

5. Close the Excel worksheet.

6. If necessary, customize your chart appearance.

    *   On the Chart Tools Design contextual tab, in the Chart Layout group, click the More button to select a layout from the gallery.

    *   On the Chart Tools Design contextual tab, in the Chart Styles group, click the More button to select a style from the gallery.

    *   On the Chart Tools Layout contextual tab, customize the labels, axes, and background of the chart.

    *   On the Chart Tools Format contextual tab, in the Shape Styles group, change the fill style, outline style, or visual effects of the shapes in the chart.

    *   On the Chart Tools Format contextual tab, in the WordArt Styles group, change the fill style, outline style, or visual effects of the text in the chart.

7. If desired, add a title to the chart.

    a. On the Layout contextual tab, in the Labels group, click Chart Title and choose a position for the chart title.

- Choose Centered Overlay to center the title over the chart without altering the chart size.

- Choose Above Chart to display the title over the chart and alter the chart size to accommodate it.

    b. If necessary, click More Title Options to display additional formatting options.

    c. In the chart, in the Chart Title text box, type the desired title.

8. If desired, add axis titles.

    a. On the Layout contextual tab, in the Labels group, click Axis Titles.

    b. From the Primary Horizontal Axis Title submenu, choose Title Below Axis to display the title below the horizontal axis.

    c. From the Primary Vertical Axis Title submenu, choose the desired option to add a title for the Y axis: Rotated Title, Vertical Title, or Horizontal Title.

    d. If necessary, from the Depth Axis Title submenu, choose the desired option to add a title for the Z axis: Default Axis for the default order with labels; Axis Without Labeling; or Reverse Axis.

    e. For each axis title, in the Axis Title text box, type the desired title.

9. To format titles, legends, or legend entries, right-click the object and use the formatting palette and menu that appear to make the necessary changes.

ACTIVITY 2-4

Creating a Chart

Data Files:

Charts.docx

Before You Begin:

From C:\084894Data\Customizing Tables and Charts, open Charts.docx.

Scenario:

Your company has registered record sales during the first four months of its initiation. You want to include the details related to these sales in the document that you are going to submit to your manager. The data is presently in a table, but you wish to present it visually to better highlight the relationship between the sales figures.

What You Do	How You Do It
1. Insert a chart in the document.	a. In the Charts document, **click the last paragraph mark at the bottom of the page.**
	b. On the Insert tab, in the Illustrations group, **click Chart.**
	c. In the Insert Chart dialog box, **verify that the first column chart type, Clustered Column, is selected and click OK.**

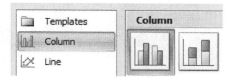

2.   Update the data in the worksheet.

a.   In the Chart In Microsoft Office Word - Microsoft Excel window, **drag to select the contents of the default table.**

b.   **Press Delete** to delete the contents of the default table.

c.   In the Charts document, **select the table.**

d.   In the Word window, on the Home tab, in the Clipboard group, **click the Copy button.**

e.   In the Chart In Microsoft Office Word - Microsoft Excel window, **click cell A1.**

f.   In the Excel window, on the Home tab, in the Clipboard group, **click Paste** to insert the table into the Excel sheet.

g.   **Close the Chart In Microsoft Office Word document.**

3.   Change the chart type.

a.   In the Charts document, **click the chart area** to select the chart.

b.   On the Chart Tools Design contextual tab, in the Type group, **click Change Chart Type.**

c.   In the Change Chart Type dialog box, in the right pane, in the Column section, in the second row, fifth column, **select Clustered Cone and click OK.**

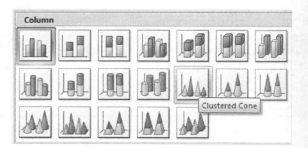

4.   Add a title to the chart.

a.   On the Chart Tools Layout contextual tab, in the Labels group, **click Chart Title and choose Above Chart** to display the chart title above the chart.

b.   The chart title text box is automatically selected for editing. **Type *SALES DATA (In millions)***

5. Specify the X and Y axis titles.

a. On the Chart Tools Layout contextual tab, in the Labels group, **click Axis Titles.**

b. **Choose Primary Horizontal Axis Title→ Title Below Axis.**

c. With the Axis Title text box selected, **type Month**

d. On the Chart Tools Layout contextual tab, in the Labels group, **click Axis Titles.**

e. **Choose Primary Vertical Axis Title→ Horizontal Title.**

f. With the Axis Title text box selected, **type (In dollars)**

g. **Click anywhere in the chart area** to deselect the title.

6. Customize the chart legend.

a. The chart legend has a third unnecessary entry. **Click the legend** to select it.

b. **Click the marker for the third legend entry** to select it.

c. **Delete the marker for the third legend entry.**

d. **Save the document as *My Charts.docx* and close it.**

Lesson 2 Follow-up

In this lesson, you customized tables and charts. Customizing a table enables you to arrange, structure, and format it to display data in the most effective way. By adding charts, you can display the information in the table graphically to enhance the impact of the figures.

1. **What kind of tables and charts have you seen in the business documents that you work with? How can you improve their appearance using the customization features?**

2. **Can you think of any documents you are working with now that you might add charts to?**

3 | Customizing Formatting with Styles and Themes

Lesson Time: 40 minutes

Lesson Objectives:

In this lesson, you will customize formatting with styles and themes.

You will:

- Create or modify a text style.
- Create a custom list or table style.
- Apply default and customized document themes.

Introduction

In the last lesson, you enhanced the basic appearance of tables by customizing tables and charts in your document. Similarly, you can enhance basic formatting of your document overall by customizing document styles and themes. In this lesson, you will customize formatting with styles and themes.

Your business probably has a communications standard that defines a unique look for your documents. It might take some time to produce custom documents if you apply each format manually. If you find yourself applying the same custom formatting repeatedly in different documents, then creating your own styles can make your life easier. Custom styles give your documents the consistent, customized formatting you need with just a few clicks of the mouse.

TOPIC A
Create or Modify a Text Style

In this lesson, you will customize formatting with styles and themes. The most fundamental category of styles that you can customize are text styles. In this topic, you will create a customized text style.

When you work with various formatting options, you increase your expertise with character and paragraph formatting. With such expertise, you may start developing a unique look for your documents by creating your own custom combinations of formats. What you will need is an easy method to apply your customized format combinations all the time. You can do this in Word by creating your own custom style.

Types of Text Styles

In Microsoft Word, there are three main types of styles that you can apply to text.

Type of Text Style	Description
Character Style	A *character style* is a style that is used to control the appearance of selected text within a paragraph. It is also called an inline style. A character style is used to format the font size, font style, font effects, character spacing, text borders, and shading of text. Additionally, it can be used to change the language settings. It does not include any paragraph-specific formatting.
Paragraph Style	A *paragraph style* is a style that can include both character formats, such as font settings, and paragraph formatting, such as paragraph alignment and indents. Paragraph styles are applied to entire paragraphs.
Linked Style	A *linked style* is a style that, like a paragraph style, contains both character and paragraph formatting but, like a character style, can be applied to a selected range of text, and not just to the paragraph as a whole.

Built-in Styles

Word includes many built-in styles, which cannot be deleted. The most commonly used styles, the built-in Heading 1, Heading 2, and Heading 3 styles, are paragraph styles. There are only a few built-in character styles. One built-in character style is called Emphasis. It italicizes the default font for the selected text.

Character Spacing

Definition:

Character spacing is a specialized formatting technique you can include in documents or incorporate into styles that controls the size of characters and the distance between them. It alters the appearance of characters by modifying the spacing and position of the selected letters by a set amount or by a percentage. You can also expand or condense individual characters.

Example:

Character Spacing Options

There are four character spacing options available on the Character Spacing tab in the Fonts dialog box.

Character Spacing Option	Description
Scale	Increases or decreases character size proportionately by a given percentage.
Spacing	Expands or condenses all the characters evenly by a given number of *points*.
Position	Raises or lowers the text in relation to the default baseline by a given number of points. It differs from superscript or subscript because it does not change the font size.
Kerning	Expands or condenses individual pairs of letters to create the appearance of even spacing. The effects of kerning are visible only in fairly large fonts, so kerning is applied only to characters above a given number of points.

Custom Styles

Definition:

A *custom style* is a style in which the formatting characteristics are defined by the user. A unique name differentiates a custom style from other predefined styles. A custom style has a combination of two or more formatting characteristics. It can be any one of the standard style types. A custom style is used when predefined styles are not sufficient to enhance the text. The custom style can be created from formatted text or be based on an existing style.

Example:

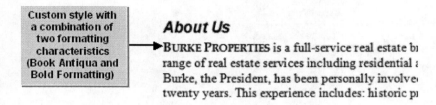

Templates in Word

Definition:

A *template* is a predefined Word document that is used as a basis for creating other new documents. Every document in Word is based on a template. Templates provide the basic structure, layout, formatting, and special characteristics for a document by storing styles and other document elements, such as the default document font, page layout settings, and boilerplate text. Most templates have the .dotx extension; if the template contains macros, which are automated series of commands, the template has a .dotm extension. There are two types of templates: *document templates*, which are used to create specific document types, and *global templates*, which store settings that are available to all open documents.

Example:

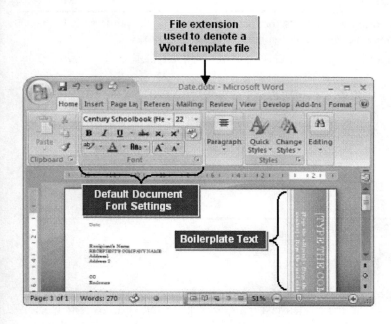

Default Document and Global Templates

Word provides many document template types. For example, Word provides templates to create various types of standard business documents, such as letters and memos.

By contrast, the Normal template (Normal.dotm) is the only default global template. By default, all new documents you open will be based on the Normal template, and changes to the Normal template will affect all documents. However, it is possible to load other document templates as global templates.

The Create New Style From Formatting Dialog Box

The Create New Style From Formatting dialog box provides options to customize text styles in Word.

Style Option	Enables You To
Name	Specify a unique name for the style.
Style Type	Set the type of style. It can be a character, paragraph, linked, list, or table style.
Style Based On	Specify any existing format that the style should be based on.
Style For Following Paragraph	Specify a particular paragraph style that will always follow the custom style.
Formatting	Set basic formatting options based on the style type.
	● For characters: font style, color, and size.
	● For paragraphs: paragraph alignment, indents, and spacing.
	● For tables: line style, and borders and shading for each portion of the table.
	● For lists: the numbering, bullets, symbols, and pictures for each level of the list.
Preview area	Preview the formatting changes before applying them.

Style Option	Enables You To
Format button	Set advanced formatting options for fonts, paragraphs, tabs, borders, and other advanced formatting settings in the appropriate dialog boxes.
Add To Quick Style List	Add a customized paragraph or character style to the Quick Style gallery.
Automatically Update	Modify a paragraph style automatically any time the text that uses the style is reformatted.
Only In the Document	Save the style only in the document that is currently in use.
New Documents Based On This Template	Make the style available in other new documents based on the current template.

Style Modification Options

You can modify styles after you have applied them to documents. You can either change the formatting in the document and then use the Styles task pane to update the style to match the text, or you can edit the style's settings directly by using the Modify Style dialog box. When you modify a style, the changes apply to any text that uses the style.

How to Create or Modify a Text Style

Procedure Reference: Create a Custom Text Style

To create a custom text style:

1. If you have formatted text to use as a basis for the style, select the text.
2. On the Home tab, in the Styles group, click the Dialog Box Launcher button to display the Styles task pane.
3. Click the New Style button to open the Create New Style From Formatting dialog box.
4. In the Name text box, type a unique new name for the style.
5. From the Style Type drop-down list, select the style type.
6. From the Style Based On drop-down list, select an existing style on which to base the new style. The default is the Normal style.
7. If you have selected a paragraph or linked style, from the Style For Following Paragraph drop-down list, select an existing style that needs to be followed by the custom style.
8. Specify the basic formatting settings in the Formatting section. The choices will vary, depending upon whether you are creating a character or paragraph style.
9. To set advanced formatting options, click Format, select a category, set the options, and click OK.
10. Select the New Documents Based On This Template option if you want the style to be available in other new documents based on the current template.
11. Click OK to create the new style.
12. To apply the style, select the appropriate section of the document and select the style from the Styles task pane or the Styles gallery.
13. To apply the style in another existing document, copy some text with the style into the other document and save the document.

Deleting a Custom Style

If you need to delete a custom style, click the drop-down arrow for the style in the Styles task pane and select Delete. Text formatted with the style will revert either to the Normal style, or to whatever other style was originally applied to the selection. You cannot delete built-in styles.

Procedure Reference: Modify Character Spacing

To modify character spacing:

1. Select the text you want to format.
2. Open the Font dialog box and select the Character Spacing tab.
3. On the Character Spacing tab, select the desired character spacing options to adjust the scale, spacing, position, and kerning of characters.
4. Verify your selections in the Preview box and click OK.

Procedure Reference: Modify a Default or Custom Style

To modify a default or custom style:

1. Open the Styles task pane.
2. If you have existing formatted text to base the style on, update the style to match the text.
   a. Select the text.
   b. Click the drop-down arrow next to the name of the style you want to modify, or right-click the style, and choose Update *<style name>* To Match Selection.
3. Make any additional manual style modifications.
   a. Click the drop-down arrow next to the name of the style you want to modify, or right-click the style, and choose Modify.
   b. Make the desired changes in the Modify Style dialog box and click OK.

Modify a Style in Other Documents

If you modify a style in a document, the modifications are applied to all text formatted with that style in the current document. However, it does not update text in other documents that are formatted with that style. One way to update the style in another document is to delete the older style in the other document. Then, copy some text formatted with the modified style to the other document.

ACTIVITY 3-1

Creating a Custom Text Style

Data Files:

Formatted Flyer.docx

Before You Begin:

From C:\084894Data\Customizing Formatting, open Formatted Flyer.docx.

Scenario:

You are working on a brochure and you want to set off the text "Burke Properties" wherever it appears. You have formatted the first item the way you want it, but you think it is going to take a long time to apply it manually everywhere else.

What You Do	How You Do It
1. **Create a custom style based on the specially formatted text.**	a. In the first line of the first paragraph, **select the text "BURKE PROPERTIES".**
	About·Our·Firm¶
	Founded·in·1946·by·John·Burke,·BURKE·PROPERTIES·is·a·full-service·re: Not·only·do·we·buy·and·sell·residential·and·commercial· properties,·Burk also·handle·your·leasing·and·relocation·needs.¶
	b. On the Home tab, in the Styles group, **click the Dialog Box Launcher button.**
	c. In the Styles task pane, **click the New Style button.**
	d. In the Create New Style From Formatting dialog box, in the Name text box, **type *BP Style***
	e. From the Style Type drop-down list, **select Character.**

f.   In the Style Based On drop-down list,
     **verify that style will be based on the
     Default Paragraph Font.**

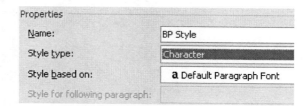

g.   Below the preview box, **verify that the
     style will include the custom formatting
     from the selection.**

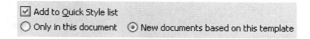

h.   **Verify that the Add To Quick Style List
     check box is checked and select the
     New Documents Based On This Tem-
     plate option** to make the style available in
     other new documents.

i.   **Click OK** to add the BP Style to the
     Styles task pane and the Styles group.

j.   **Close the Styles task pane.**

2.   **Apply the new style to the other
     instances of the text "Burke Prop-
     erties" in the document.**

a.   In the second line of the first paragraph,
     select the text "Burke Properties".

b.   In the Styles pane, **select BP Style** to
     apply the style to the selected text.

c.   In the first line of the second paragraph,
     select the text "Burke Properties".

d.   In the Styles pane, **select BP Style** to
     apply the style to the text.

3. **Change the character spacing in the first occurrence of the text "Burke Properties".**

    a. In the first line of the first paragraph, **select the text "BURKE PROPERTIES".**

    b. In the Font group, **click the Font dialog box launcher and select the Character Spacing tab.**

    c. From the Spacing drop-down list, **select Expanded.**

    d. In the Preview section, observe that the text has been expanded by 1 pt and **click OK.**

    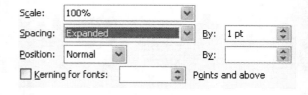

4. **Modify the custom style to match the new formatting.**

    a. **Verify that the text is still selected.**

    b. In the Styles task pane, **move the mouse pointer over the BP Style** to view the drop-down arrow.

    c. **Click the BP Style drop-down arrow and select Update BP Style To Match Selection.**

d. **Verify that the BP Style has been updated with the new format in all sections of the document.**

Founded·in·1946·by·John·Burke,·BURKE·PROPERTIES·is·a·full-service·real·estate·
agency.·Not·only·do·we·buy·and·sell·residential·and·commercial·properties,·BURKE·
PROPERTIES·can·also·handle·your·leasing·and·relocation·needs.¶
¶
In·the·last·10·years,·BURKE·PROPERTIES·has·expanded·tremendously,·opening·branch·

e. **Close the Styles task pane.**

f. **Save the document as *My Burke Flyer.docx* and close the document.**

TOPIC B
Create a Custom List or Table Style

In the previous topic, you worked with character and paragraph styles that allowed you to format plain text. For text that is in the form of lists or tables, you will need to create styles that give you a way to incorporate and apply all the desired formatting settings for those items. In this topic, you will create a list or table style.

Once you see the value of creating and saving custom styles for the general text in your document, you might find that you want to create styles for specific document elements, such as lists and tables. These document components have specialized, highly customizable formatting options that go beyond those available in character and paragraph styles. If you have a customized list and table appearance to suit your preferences, you can create and save the formats in custom styles for those document elements as a way to ensure consistency of appearance in your work and to save yourself time.

List and Table Style Tools

You can use the Create New Style From Formatting dialog box to create list and table styles. Once you specify the appropriate style type, you will have access to the style options for that document component, such as bullet characters for different levels of lists, or cell borders for all or part of a table. If you select a formatted list in a document and then open the dialog box, you will see the existing list formats; however, even if you select a formatted table, you will still need to set up all the table formatting for the style by hand.

Another tool you can use to create a list style is the Define New List Style dialog box, available from the Multilevel List gallery. The list-style formatting options in this dialog box are the same as those in the Create New Style From Formatting dialog box.

How to Create a Custom List or Table Style

Procedure Reference: Create a Custom List Style

To create a custom list style:

1. If you have a formatted list you want to use as the basis for the new style, select the list.
2. Open the appropriate dialog box.
    -   Open the Create New Style From Formatting dialog box and choose List as the style type.
    -   Or, on the Home tab, in the Paragraph group, click the Multilevel List drop-down button and select Define New List Style.
3. In the Name text box, type a unique new name for the style.
4. If necessary, from the Apply Formatting To drop-down list, specify the list level to which the formatting should be applied.
5. For a numbered list level, in the Start At spin box, specify the number with which the level of the list should begin.
6. In the Formatting section, set the basic formatting options for the current level of the list.
7. Click Format to set any advanced formatting options for the current level of the list.
8. When you are finished formatting each level of the list, select the next level you want to format and configure the settings for that level.

9. Select the New Documents Based On This Template option, if you want the style to be available in other new documents.

10. Click OK to create the new style.

11. Test the style by applying it to any desired list.

Procedure Reference: Create a Custom Table Style

To create a custom table style:

1. If you have an existing formatted table that you want to use as the basis for the new style, select the table.

2. Display the Create New Style From Formatting dialog box.
   - In the Styles task pane, click the New Style button.
   - Or, on the Table Tools Design contextual tab, click the More button and select New Table Style.

3. In the Name text box, type a unique new name for the style.

4. If necessary, from the Style Type drop-down list, select Table.

5. From the Style Based On drop-down list, select any existing table style that you want to base this style on. The default is Table Normal.

6. From the Apply Formatting To drop-down list, select the portion of the table you want to apply formatting to.

7. In the Formatting section, set the basic formatting options for this portion of the table.

8. Click Format to set any advanced formatting options for this portion of the table.

9. When you are finished formatting each section of the table, select the next section you want to format and configure the settings for that section.

10. Select the New Documents Based On This Template option if you want the style to be available in other new documents.

11. Click OK to create the new style.

12. Test the style by applying it to any desired table.

ACTIVITY 3-2
Creating a List Style

Data Files:

List Style.docx

Before You Begin:

From C:\084894Data\Customizing Formatting, open List Style.docx.

Scenario:

As the Human Resources Manager for Burke Properties, you find that you often create lists of instructions that have a similar format—a numbered list with a second level of bulleted items. You have been customizing each of your lists manually to achieve this appearance, but this is very time consuming.

What You Do	How You Do It
1. **Create a list style based on the list in the document.**	a. **Select all the list items from item 1 through 5.**
	b. On the Home tab, in the Paragraph group, **click the Multilevel List button and select Define New List Style.**
	c. In the Define New List Style dialog box, in the Name text box, **type My BP List**
	d. **Select the New Documents Based On This Template option** to make the style available in other new documents.
	e. **Click OK** to create the style and close the dialog box.
	f. **Save the document as My List Style.docx and close the document.**

2. Test the list style.

a. **Click the Office button and choose New.**

b. In the New Document dialog box, in the right pane, **verify that Blank Document is selected and then click Create** to create a new blank document.

c. In the Paragraph group, **click the Multilevel List button.**

d. In the List Styles section, **select the My BP List style.**

e. In the document, **type *first line* and press Enter.**

f. **Press Tab** to demote this paragraph and apply the bullet style for the second list level.

g. **Type *second level* and press Enter.**

h. **Save the document as *My List Test.docx* and close the document.**

ACTIVITY 3-3
Creating a Table Style

Data Files:

Mortgage Table.docx

Before You Begin:

From C:\084894data\Customizing Formatting, open Mortgage Table.docx.

Scenario:

As an agent for Burke Properties, you often create tables of information that have a similar format. You have been customizing each of your tables manually to achieve this appearance, but this is time consuming. You want to set up the formatting once so that you can apply it to any table.

What You Do	How You Do It
1. **Specify the style name.**	a. In the table in the document, **click the word "Location"** to activate the Table Tools contextual tab.
	b. On the Table Tools Design contextual tab, in the Table Styles group, **click the More button and select New Table Style** to display the Create New Style From Formatting dialog box.
	c. In the Name text box, **type *BP Table***
	d. In the Style Based On drop-down list, **verify that Table Normal is selected by default.**

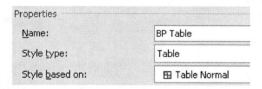

2. Format the header row.

a. From the Apply Formatting To drop-down list, **select Header Row.**

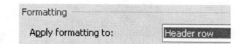

b. **Click the Bold button and preview the header row format.**

	Jan	Feb	Mar	Total
East	7	7	5	19
West	6	4	7	17
South	8	7	9	24
Total	21	18	21	60

c. **Click the drop-down arrow next to the alignment button** [≡ ▾] **and click the Align Center button.**

d. **Click the Fill Color drop-down arrow** to view the gallery.

e. In the Standard Colors section, **click the seventh color from the left** to select the light blue color.

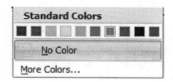

3. Add borders to the whole table.

a. From the Apply Formatting To drop-down list, **select Whole Table.**

b. **Click the All Borders button** [⊞] to add borders to the table.

4. Save the style.

a. **Select the New Documents Based On This Template option.**

b. **Click OK** to create the table style.

5. **Apply the BP Table style to the table.**

a. With any part of the table selected, on the Table Tools Design contextual tab, in the Table Styles group, **select the BP Table style**, which is the first style.

Location	Rate (%)	As of:
Atlanta, GA	6.75	July 9, 2007
Boston, MA	6.77	July 15, 2007
Chicago, IL	6.96	July 11, 2007
Denver, CO	6.82	July 9, 2007
Los Angeles, CA	6.73	July 11, 2007
Miami, FL	6.79	July 12, 2007
New York, NY	6.86	July 6, 2007
Philadelphia, PA	6.71	July 12, 2007
Rochester, NY	6.13	July 8, 2007
Seattle, WA	6.77	July 13, 2007
Washington, DC	6.63	July 15, 2007

b. **Save the document as *My Mortgage Table.docx* and close the document.**

TOPIC C
Apply Default and Customized Document Themes

In the first topics of this lesson, you used styles to efficiently apply consistent formatting to different elements of a document. You can use document themes in a similar manner to apply consistent font, color, and style effects across all the pages of a document. In this topic, you will apply document themes.

If you want to create a document that looks the same as one you created earlier, trying to re-create the formatting of the existing document would take a lot of time and effort. By using document themes, you can recreate and apply consistent formatting styles across documents in a matter of seconds.

Document Themes

Definition:

Document themes are sets of formatting options that can be applied to the entire document to ensure a consistent look. Themes are stored in files with an extension of .thmx. A theme controls the available styles, colors, fonts, and effects for the elements that are inserted into the document. There are several predefined document themes provided in Word. You can either pick an existing theme for your document, or you can create your own theme by customizing an existing theme. The newly created theme can be saved in a theme file and applied to other documents.

Example:

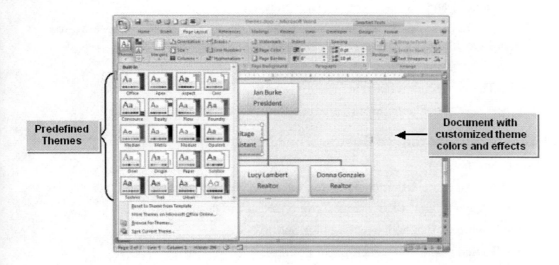

The Themes Group

The Themes group on the Page Layout tab has formatting options that can be applied to the entire document.

Option	Description
Theme Colors	Displays a gallery of color options, which can be applied to a theme. The Create New Theme Colors option allows for the creation of custom colors for a theme.
Theme Fonts	Displays a gallery of font options, which can be applied to a theme. The Create New Theme Fonts option allows for the creation of custom fonts for a theme.
Theme Effects	Displays a gallery of effects, which can be applied to a theme. Effects include lines and fill effects, which can be applied to the graphics inserted in the document.

How to Apply Default and Customized Document Themes

Procedure Reference: Apply Document Themes

To apply document themes:

1. Open the Word document to which you want to apply a theme.
2. On the Page Layout tab, in the Themes group, click Themes.
3. In the Built-In gallery, select a theme to apply it to the document.
4. If necessary, browse for more themes.
    *   Click Themes and choose Browse For Themes.
    *   Or, if you have an Internet connection, you can click Themes and choose More Themes On Microsoft Office Online.
5. If necessary, restore the template theme.
    a. In the Themes group, click Themes.
    b. Choose Reset To Theme From Template to revert back to the template theme.

Procedure Reference: Create a Custom Theme

To create a custom theme:

1. Open the Word document that contains the theme to be customized.
2. On the Page Layout tab, in the Themes group, select the desired formats.
    *   Click Theme Colors and select a color option.
    *   Click Theme Fonts and select a font option.
    *   Click Theme Effects and select an effect.
3. Save the theme.
    a. In the Themes group, click Themes.
    b. Choose Save Current Theme.
    c. In the Save Current Theme dialog box, in the File Name text box, type the desired name and click Save.

Procedure Reference: Delete a Custom Theme

To delete a custom theme:

1. On the Page Layout tab, in the Themes group, click Themes to display the Themes gallery.

2. Delete the custom theme.

   ● Right-click the theme in the gallery, choose Delete, and in the Microsoft Office Word dialog box, click Yes.

   ● Or, click Save Current Theme, select the theme file, click Tools, and select Delete.

Setting a Default Theme

In Word, the theme is closely tied to the Quick Style set you are using so that you set the default theme at the same time that you set the default style set. If you want to choose a different theme to use as your default, you should first open a document and select the desired theme. Then, on the Home tab, in the Styles group, choose Change Styles→Style Set, and select a Quick Style set from the list. Then, to set both the selected Quick Style set and the current theme as the Word defaults, choose Change Styles→Set As Default.

ACTIVITY 3-4
Applying Default and Customized Document Themes

Data Files:

Themes.docx

Before You Begin:

From C:\084894Data\Customizing Formatting, open Themes.docx.

Scenario:

You need to prepare a document on the sales data of your junior sales associates. You want to give your document a professional look by applying formatting options to the text and graphics in the document. Since you may need to apply this formatting to other documents later, you want to save the chosen settings.

What You Do	How You Do It
1. Apply a default document theme.	a. On the Page Layout tab, in the Themes group, **click Themes,** and in the gallery, **select Median** to apply the theme to the document.
2. Customize the theme.	a. In the Themes group, **click the Theme Colors button.**
	b. In the gallery, in the Built-In section, **select Concourse** to change the default theme color set.
	c. **Click the Theme Fonts button** and in the gallery, in the Built-in section, **scroll down and select Foundry** to change the theme font set.
	d. In the Themes - Microsoft Word window, **scroll down to the second page.**
	e. On the Page Layout tab, in the Themes group, **click the Theme Effects button.**
	f. The graphic object has an effect applied. In the gallery, in the Built-In section, **select Opulent** to change the theme effects set.

3.   Save the custom theme.

a.   On the Page Layout tab, in the Themes group, **click Themes and choose Save Current Theme.**

b.   In the Save Current Theme dialog box, in the File Name text box, **type *My Theme1* and click Save.**

c.   On the Page Layout tab, in the Themes group, **click Themes.**

d.   In the gallery, in the Custom section, **verify that the custom theme has been added to the Custom gallery.**

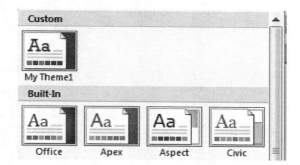

e.   **Click anywhere in the document** to close the gallery.

f.   **Save the document as *My Themes.docx* and close it.**

Lesson 3 Follow-up

In this lesson, you customized styles and themes for document elements. Custom styles and themes enable you to create the professional formatting you need for documents and apply the formatting quickly and consistently.

1.   **Can you think of situations where you might need to combine several formats to create a custom look?**

2.   **How would using a custom style make formatting a document easier for you?**

4 | Modifying Pictures

Lesson Time: 35 minutes

Lesson Objectives:

In this lesson, you will modify pictures in a document.

You will:

- Resize a picture.
- Adjust picture appearance settings.
- Wrap text around a picture.

Introduction

In the previous lesson, you used styles and themes to customize the overall look of your document. You can also customize the appearance of individual components within your documents, such as pictures and Clip Art. In this lesson, you will modify pictures in your documents.

You don't have to be an artist to add captivating graphics to your document. You can put an existing graphic, such as a Word Clip Art element, into your document quickly and easily to add visual interest. You don't have to stop there; you can also modify the default appearance of the pictures you insert to create a custom look.

TOPIC A
Resize a Picture

In this lesson, you will modify pictures. A simple and common way to modify a picture is to use one of several different methods to change its overall size. In this topic, you will resize a picture.

Do you have a square picture to fit into a long, thin, empty spot in your document? Do you like the boat in the picture, but don't want to show the dock? Or do you have a picture with too much grass, but not enough sky? Word has options to resize the picture to fit your requirements.

Resizing Options

There are four basic options you can use to change the size of a picture.

Option	Use This To
Size	Change the height and width of the picture by specific values. This option retains all the content of the picture and stretches the picture in a given direction.
Rotate	Adjust the angle of the picture by a given degree of rotation. Although this does not affect the overall size of the picture, the angle of rotation can affect the amount of text that can fit around the picture on a page.
Scale	Change the height and width of the picture by percentages. This option retains all the content of the picture and changes the size proportionately.
Crop	Change the size of the picture by removing content from the picture. You can trim the picture from the left, right, top, or bottom. You can also add white space around the picture by specifying a negative cropping value.

How to Resize a Picture

Procedure Reference: Crop a Picture with the Crop Button

To crop a picture with the Crop button:

1. Select the picture.
2. On the Picture Tools Format contextual tab, in the Size group, click the Crop button.
3. Cropping handles appear around the picture and the mouse pointer changes to a cropping tool shape when placed near these handles. Drag the cropping handles in the desired direction to crop the picture appropriately.
4. Click the Crop button again to turn off the cropping handles and the cropping tool.

Procedure Reference: Modify a Picture with the Size Dialog Box

To modify a picture with the Size dialog box:

1. Select the picture.
2. In the Size group, click the Dialog Box Launcher button to display the Size dialog box.
3. If you need to set an exact size, in the Size And Rotate section, set the Height and Width values in inches. It might be useful to compare the size values to the original picture size that appears at the bottom of the dialog box.
4. If you need to rotate the picture to a specific angle, in the Rotation text box, enter the degree of rotation.
5. If you need to scale the picture by a percentage in either direction, in the Scale section, enter the Height and Width percentages, and select Additional Scaling Options.
   - Uncheck the Lock Aspect Ratio check box if you want the height and width to scale separately and not proportionately with each other.
   - Uncheck the Relative To Original Picture Size check box if you want to scale the picture relative to its current size and not relative to its original size.
6. If you need to crop the picture, set the desired values in the Crop From section to crop the picture from the left, right, top, or bottom. Set negative values to add white space.
7. Click Close.

 Remember that you can resize or rotate the picture to approximate values by selecting the picture in the document and dragging the appropriate sizing handles.

ACTIVITY 4-1
Resizing a Picture

Data Files:

Picture Flyer.docx

Before You Begin:

From C:\084894Data\Modifying Pictures, open Picture Flyer.docx.

Scenario:

You are preparing a promotional flyer to help clients understand and appreciate the company's history and values. A picture will help set the right mood. However, the picture you have is too big to fit with text on the page and has been snapped in the vertical position. Also, you want the focus of the picture to be on the house, rather than on the landscape that surrounds it.

What You Do	How You Do It
1. **Crop the picture to remove the extra landscape from the top and right side of the picture.**	a. **Scroll down to the second page of the document and select the picture.**
	b. On the Picture Tools Format contextual tab, in the Size group, **click the Crop button.**
	c. **Place the mouse pointer over the center handle on the right border of the picture.**
	d. **Click and drag the crop tool pointer toward the left until the border touches the roof of the house.**
	e. **Place the mouse pointer over the center handle on the top border of the picture.**
	f. **Click and drag the crop tool pointer downward until the border touches the roof of the house.**
	g. Because the picture is smaller, it now fits on the first page. **Scroll up** to view the picture on the first page.
	h. If the crop handles are still visible, **click the Crop button** to turn off the cropping tool.

2. Resize the picture to fit along with the text.

a. On the Picture Tools Format contextual tab, in the Size group, **click the Dialog Box Launcher button** to launch the Size dialog box.

b. On the Size tab, in the Scale section, **verify that the Lock Aspect Ratio and Relative To Original Picture Size check boxes are checked** to scale the picture proportionately.

c. In the Scale section, in the Height text box, **type 40** to scale the picture to 40 percent of its prior size.

d. **Press Tab** to automatically set the Width scaling value to 40%.

3. Rotate the picture to a horizontal orientation.

a. In the Size And Rotate section, in the Rotation text box, **type 270** to spin the picture to horizontal view.

b. **Click Close** to save the changes.

c. **Scroll to the top of the document** to verify the changes.

d. **Save the document as *My Picture Flyer.docx***

TOPIC B
Adjust Picture Appearance Settings

You have adjusted the size of the picture to suit your document needs. You now want to enhance a picture by modifying its contrast and brightness and creating variations in the color. In this topic, you will set picture prominence.

Being able to set a picture's contrast and brightness and other appearance settings means you have the ability to control how prominent a picture is on the page. The statement your picture makes can be bold or subtle; it can be in the foreground or the background; it can grab attention or just lend atmosphere. Picture settings such as contrast, brightness, and coloration can help you achieve these effects.

The Adjust Group

The Adjust group, on the Picture Tools Format tab, has options that enable you to enhance the appearance of a picture by changing various technical properties. You can change the picture's brightness, contrast, and overall color scheme; change the picture's color format to reduce the file size of the document; replace the picture with another one; and also revert the picture to its original state.

Picture Contrast

Definition:

Picture contrast is an image-control setting that controls the amount of difference between adjacent colors or shades of gray in the graphic element. Contrast is set as a percentage. A picture with no contrast will be gray. A picture with 100 percent contrast will contain only black, white, and primary colors. The contrast setting does not affect the portions of the picture that are pure white.

Example:

Original Image

Image with no contrast   Image with 100% contrast

Picture Brightness

Definition:

Picture brightness is an image-control setting that changes the amount of white present in the colors or shades of gray in the graphic element. Brightness is set as a percentage. A picture with no brightness will be black, except for those portions of the image that were pure white. A picture with 100 percent brightness will be white. The brightness setting does not affect the portions of the picture that are pure white.

Example:

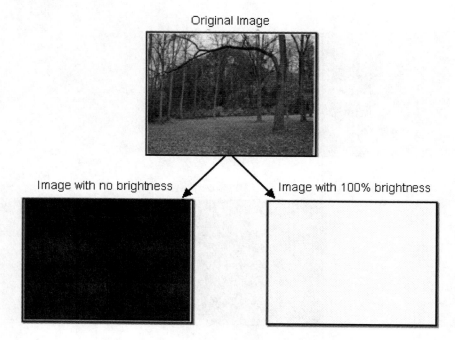

The Recolor Gallery

The Recolor gallery, available from the Recolor button in the Adjust group, displays options you can use to modify the color shade of a picture. The Color Modes section in the gallery displays the picture in different effects, such as Grayscale, Sepia, Washout, and Black and White. The Dark Variations and Light Variations sections of the gallery display the picture in dark or light color variations and with additional color tints. You can also restore the original coloring of the picture using the No Recolor option. The last section of the gallery enables you to select colors from the document's theme, and to make a selected color in the picture transparent.

Compression

Definition:

Compression is a method of reducing the file size by using fewer bits to store the same amount of information. For graphics, compression changes the color format so that the computer requires less information to store each individual dot, or *pixel* of color. If you have files that take up a lot of space because they contain large or complex graphics, you can compress one or more of the graphics within the files to reduce the overall amount of storage space that the file requires.

 ppi stands for "pixels per inch."

Example:

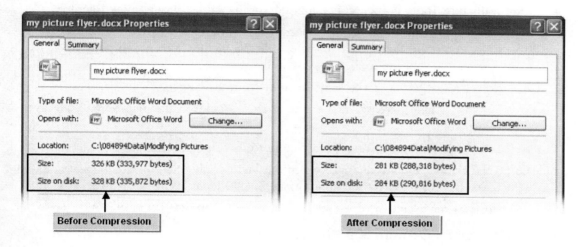

Compression Options

Word compresses all pictures by a standard amount when you save a file; you can select specific compression options based on your intended use for the document that contains the pictures:

- The Print (220 ppi) setting will compress the picture slightly but maintain print output quality.

- The Screen (150 ppi) setting will compress the picture a moderate amount but retain visual quality.

- The E-mail (96 ppi) setting will compress the picture as much as possible to minimize the file size.

How to Adjust Picture Appearance Settings

Procedure Reference: Adjust Picture Appearance

To adjust picture appearance:

1. Select the picture.
2. To apply a Quick Style to the picture, on the Picture Tools Format contextual tab, in the Picture Styles group, select a style from the gallery.
3. Set the brightness value.

    - On the Picture Tools Format contextual tab, in the Adjust group, click the Brightness button and select a percentage from the gallery.

    - Or, to set a specific value, on the Picture Tools Format contextual tab, in the Picture Styles group, click the Dialog Box Launcher button to open the Format Picture dialog box. On the Picture tab, drag the brightness slider or type a percentage and click Close.

4. Set the contrast value.

    - On the Picture Tools Format contextual tab, in the Adjust group, click the Contrast button and select a percentage from the gallery.

    - Or, to set a specific value, open the Format Picture dialog box. On the Picture tab, drag the contrast slider or type a percentage and click Close.

5. Recolor the picture.
   - On the Picture Tools Format contextual tab, in the Adjust group, click Recolor.
     - Select an option in the Color Modes, Dark Variations, or Light Variations sections to modify the shades and effects of the picture. When you point to the option, you will see a live preview in the document.
     - Select More Variations to select a color from the respective gallery.
     - Select Set Transparent Color and then click a color in the picture to make it transparent.
     - Select No Recolor to revert the picture to its original state.
   - Or, in the Format Picture dialog box, on the Picture tab, click the Recolor button and select No Recolor or select the appropriate Color Modes, Dark Variations, or Light Variations options from the gallery.

Procedure Reference: Compress a Picture

To compress a picture to reduce the file size of a document:

1. Select the picture.
2. On the Picture Tools Format contextual tab, in the Adjust group, click Compress Pictures.
3. In the Compress Pictures dialog box, check Apply To Selected Pictures Only.
4. If you need to modify the compression settings, click Options to open the Compression Settings dialog box.
   - Check the Automatically Perform Basic Compression On Save check box to compress the picture automatically when saving the file.
   - Check the Delete Cropped Areas Of Picture check box to delete the edited areas of the picture.
   - Select the appropriate compression level for the target output.
5. Click OK to close the Compression Settings dialog box.
6. Click OK to apply the modified options and to close the Compress Pictures dialog box.

Resetting a Picture

To reset a picture to its original appearance, select the picture, and then click Reset Picture in the Adjust group, or, in the Format Picture dialog box, on the Picture tab, click Reset Picture.

ACTIVITY 4-2

Adjusting Picture Appearance

Before You Begin:

My Picture Flyer.docx is open.

Scenario:

The promotional flyer to help clients understand and appreciate the company's history and values is ready for printing. However, you realize that the darkness and intensity of the picture will distract the reader's attention from the text. When you are done, you will need to email the file to a colleague for review, and you want the attachment size to be as small as possible.

What You Do	How You Do It
1. **Set the brightness and contrast value for the picture.**	a. If necessary, **click the picture** to select it.
	b. On the Picture Tools Format contextual tab, in the Picture Styles group, **click the Dialog Box Launcher button** to open the Format Picture dialog box.
	c. On the Picture tab, in the Brightness text box, **type 30** to change the brightness of the picture.
	d. On the Picture tab, in the Contrast text box, **type 80**

Picture

Brightness: 30% ⏶⏷

Contrast: 80% ⏶⏷

	e. **Click Close.**
2. **Recolor the picture to apply a light pink tinge to the picture.**	a. In the Adjust group, **click Recolor.**
	b. From the Recolor gallery, in the Light Variations section, **select the third color from the left.**

3. **Reduce the file size of the picture.**

a. In the Adjust group, **click Compress Pictures.**

b. In the Compress Pictures dialog box, **check the Apply To Selected Pictures Only check box** to compress the selected picture.

c. **Click Options.**

d. **Select the E-mail (96 ppi) option and click OK.**

e. **Click OK** to compress the picture and reduce the overall document file size.

f. **Save the document.**

TOPIC C
Wrap Text Around a Picture

In the previous topic, you adjusted a picture's appearance settings. Once the picture is formatted correctly, you can adjust the way the surrounding text fits with the picture. In this topic, you will wrap text around a picture.

Pictures in a document usually don't stand alone. They relate to the text by providing visual examples for the text in a document. If the text is positioned too far away from the picture, obscured by the picture, or misaligned with the picture, it might affect the readability of the document. By using the text wrapping options, you can get the best visual effect from the pictures and text in your document.

Text Wrapping Styles

Definition:

Text wrapping styles are formatting options that determine how adjacent text will appear along with a graphic. The picture can be placed inline with the text, which enables you to position the graphic within a paragraph at a selected point. Otherwise, the picture can be treated as a floating graphic, which is stored in a drawing layer separate from the text layer and can be positioned anywhere. As a floating graphic, text can wrap square to the picture, tight to the shape of the picture, or across the top and bottom of the picture. Text can flow behind or in front of the graphic, or lines of text can break so that they flow right through the graphic.

Example:

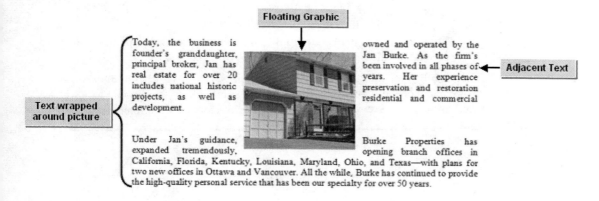

Advanced Wrapping Options

There are also some advanced text wrapping options available in the Advanced Layout dialog box. For example, you can control the amount of white space between the graphic and the text wrapped around it. You can also configure the text to wrap on one side of the picture. Some of these options cannot be applied to inline graphics.

Picture Positioning Options

Picture positioning options orient a picture vertically or horizontally in relation to a block of text, and can also set a text wrapping style. You can use basic positioning options to place a picture within a text block in a corner, on a side, or in the middle. You can also customize the picture position for fine control of the placement and behavior of the graphic.

Advanced Picture Position Options

The picture position options in the Advanced Layout box provide precise control of a picture's position.

Picture Position Settings	Description
Horizontal	These settings control the horizontal placement of the picture. ● Alignment: Provides options to align the picture to the left, right, or center relative to the page, character, column, or margins. ● Book Layout: Provides options to position the picture inside or outside of a page or margin. ● Absolute Position: Provides options to set the exact location of the picture to the right of the margin, page, column, or character. ● Relative Position: Provides options to set exact percentages for the position of the picture relative to the margins or page.
Vertical	These settings control the vertical placement of the picture. ● Alignment: Provides options to align the picture to the top, bottom, center, inside, or outside relative to the page, line, or margins. ● Absolute Position: Provides options to set the exact location of the picture below the margins, page, paragraph, or line. ● Relative Position: Provides options to set the location of the picture as a percentage value relative to the margins or page.
Options	These settings enable you to configure the object to move when the text moves, anchor the graphic in a particular position, allow the graphic to overlap the text, or control the layout of the graphic within a table.

How to Wrap Text Around a Picture

Procedure Reference: Set Position and Text Wrapping Style for a Picture

To set the position and text wrapping style for a picture:

1. Select the picture.

2. On the Picture Tools Format contextual tab, in the Arrange group, specify a position for the picture.

    • Click Position and select a preferred position.

    • Or, click Position and select More Layout Options.

    a. In the Advanced Layout dialog box, on the Picture Position tab, select the desired vertical and horizontal positions and any position options.

    b. Click OK.

3. On the Picture Tools Format contextual tab, in the Arrange group, specify a text wrapping style.

    • Click Text Wrapping and select the desired wrapping style.

    • Or, click Text Wrapping and select More Layout Options.

    a. In the Advanced Layout dialog box, on the Text Wrapping tab, select the desired wrapping style.

    b. Click OK.

ACTIVITY 4-3

Setting the Text Wrapping Style for a Picture

Before You Begin:

My Picture Flyer.docx is open.

Scenario:

Your picture's size, shape, and appearance are all set. You have to decide where to place the picture in your flyer so that it complements the text in the document.

What You Do	How You Do It
1. **Set the Square text wrapping style for the picture.**	a. **Click the picture** to select it.
	b. On the Picture Tools Format contextual tab, in the Arrange group, **click Text Wrapping.**
	c. From the Text Wrapping drop-down menu, **choose Square.**
	d. **Scroll down and verify that the picture is placed near the margin and is wrapped with text on three sides.**
2. **Position the picture to the right of the document.**	a. On the Picture Tools Format contextual tab, in the Arrange group, **click Position.**
	b. In the Position gallery, in the With Text Wrapping section, in the second row, **select Position In Middle Right With Square Text Wrapping** to place the picture at the middle-right position of the document.
	c. **Scroll down** and verify that the picture is paced at the middle-right of the document.
	d. **Click outside the picture** to deselect it.
	e. **Save the document and close it.**

Lesson 4 Follow-up

In this lesson, you modified the appearance of pictures that you inserted into your document. Whether you need to set the contrast and brightness to change the overall effect of a picture, crop the picture to fit your shape and size requirements, or set the text wrapping properties so your picture lines up properly with your text, modifying the picture enables you to customize it to suit your requirements for graphics.

1. **What are some of the effects that you have seen on graphics in the documents that you work with?**

2. **How do you think you might use the picture-modification techniques presented in this lesson?**

5 | Creating Customized Graphic Elements

Lesson Time: 50 minutes

Lesson Objectives:

In this lesson, you will create customized graphic elements.

You will:

- Create text boxes and pull quotes.
- Draw shapes.
- Add WordArt and other special text effects.
- Create complex illustrations with SmartArt.

Introduction

In the previous topic, you customized existing pictures that you inserted from files or from Clip Art. You can also create your own custom graphic objects in Word documents. In this lesson, you will create customized graphic elements.

While working with the visuals for your document, you may need customized graphics that are not available as Clip Art items or picture files. You don't have to limit yourself to the Clip Art Gallery. Whether you need to create an unusual look for your document titles, draw lines, arrows, or geometric shapes, or build personalized business diagrams, you can use Word to create your own custom graphic elements to add variety and complexity to your documents.

TOPIC A

Create Text Boxes and Pull Quotes

In this lesson, you will create customized graphic elements. Text boxes are common graphic elements that enable you to manipulate text in your document as you would a graphic object. In this topic, you will insert text boxes.

You might have an announcement in a newsletter that has to stay on page one. You might need to add some commentary next to a chart. You might need some text to fit inside a precise area of your document. Text boxes can meet your needs in all of these cases.

Text Boxes

Definition:

A *text box* is a graphic entity that serves as a container for text or other graphics. It has a clearly defined border in which the text appears. Text and graphics within the box move with it. Text in the box flows to conform to the shape of the box. You can format the text or graphics within the text box as desired. Because the text box is a graphic object, it can be moved or resized. You can also format the text box itself as you would format any other graphic object.

Example:

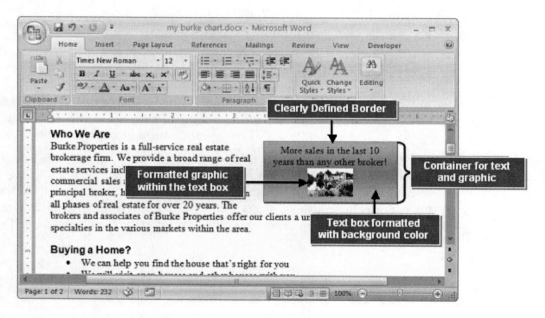

 A paragraph that is formatted with a border and shading may look like a large text box. However, you cannot move, size, rotate, or wrap other text around the paragraph as you can with a text box.

Pull Quotes and Sidebars

Definition:

Pull quotes and *sidebars* are two specialized types of predefined text boxes that are customized to appear according to common commercial publication conventions. Sidebars generally supplement the main text, and often align with the edge of the page; pull quotes generally extract and emphasize small portions of existing text. Either type can be formatted in the same way as other text boxes to suit the document. The predefined text boxes align themselves according to the formatting descriptions present in the ScreenTip. However, the predefined text boxes have tabs that enable you to move them around the document and position them according to your requirements. They can also be resized.

Example:

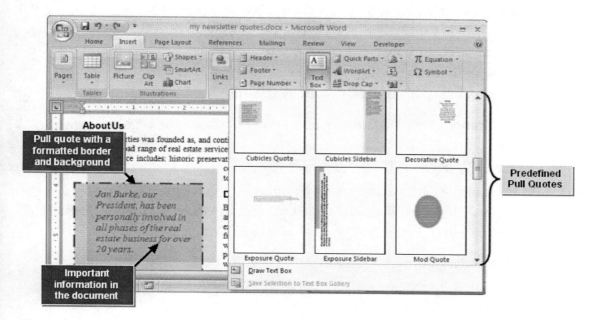

The Text Box Gallery

The Text Box gallery provides built-in pre-formatted text boxes, pull quotes, and sidebars in a variety of styles and colors. After inserting a text box, you can replace the placeholder text with the desired text. The built-in text boxes can be further formatted by using the options in the Text Box Tools Format contextual tab.

The Text Box Tools Format Contextual Tab

The Text Box Tools Format contextual tab contains different groups that provide the formatting options for a text box.

Group	Provides Options To
Text	Draw a text box, change the text flow, and link two text boxes.
Text Box Styles	Select a style, fill color, outline color, and shape for the text box.
Shadow Effects	Set the shadow effects for the text box.

Group	Provides Options To
3-D Effects	Set a 3-D effect for the text box and tilt it to any desired angle.
Arrange	Select the text wrapping, positioning, and rotation options for the text box.
Size	Set the height and width value for the text box.

How to Create Text Boxes and Pull Quotes

Procedure Reference: Draw a Text Box

To draw a text box:

1. Place the insertion point where you want the text box to appear.
2. On the Insert tab, in the Text group, click Text Box.
3. Select the Draw Text Box option.
4. Drag to draw the text box.
5. Type the text and insert any graphics you want to be displayed in the text box.

Procedure Reference: Insert a Built-in Text Box, Pull Quote or Sidebar

To insert a built-in text box, pull quote, or sidebar:

1. Place the insertion point where you want the text box.
2. On the Insert tab, in the Text group, click Text Box.
3. From the Text Box gallery, select the desired type of text box, pull quote, or sidebar.
4. Edit the default text by typing new text within the text box.

Procedure Reference: Format a Text Box

To format a text box:

1. Select the text box you want to format.
2. On the Ribbon, select the Text Box Tools Format contextual tab.
3. In the Text group, click Text Direction to change the flow of text within the box.
4. If necessary, in the Text Box Styles group, select the style, fill color, and outline options for the text box.
   - Click the More button and, from the gallery, select a text box style.
   - Click Shape Fill and select a fill color.
   - Click Shape Outline and specify the color, width, and line style of the outline.
   - Click Change Shape and select a different shape to change the shape of the text box.
5. If necessary, in the Shadow Effects group, click Shadow Effects and set the shadow effects for the text box.
6. If necessary, in the 3-D Effects group, click 3-D Effects and set the 3-D effects for the text box.
7. In the Arrange group, select the position, text wrapping, and alignment options of the text box.
8. In the Size group, set the height and width value of the text box.

ACTIVITY 5-1
Creating Text Boxes

Data Files:

Special Burke Graphics.docx

Before You Begin

From C:\084894Data\Creating Customized Graphics Elements, open Special Burke Graphics.docx.

Scenario:

Burke Properties has made more sales in the last 10 years than any other area real estate firm. You want this information to be contained within a separate entity on the page so that it does not look like just another paragraph.

What You Do	How You Do It
1. **Draw a text box in the first paragraph.**	a. Below the Who We Are sub-heading, **place the insertion point at the beginning of the paragraph.**
	b. On the Insert tab, in the Text group, **click Text Box.**
	c. From the Text Box drop-down list, **select Draw Text Box.**
	d. **Drag to draw a text box that covers the first three lines in height and about half the width of the first paragraph of text.**

Who We Are

state brokerage firm. We provide a broad sidential and commercial sales and , has been personally involved in all phases of real estate for over 20 years. The brokers and associates of Burke Properties offer our clients a unique blend of specialties in the various markets within the area.

2. **Type text in the text box.**	a. **Type *More sales in the last 10 years than any other area broker!***
	b. On the Home tab, in the Paragraph group, **click the Center button** to center the text within the box.

3. **Format the text box by applying a style.**

    a. On the Text Box Tools Format contextual tab, in the Text Box Styles group, **click the More button.**

    b. In the gallery, in the first row, **click the second style from the right, with the blue shade,** to apply it to the text box.

4. **Set the text wrapping and alignment for the text box.**

    a. **Move the mouse pointer to the top-left corner of the text box until it becomes a four-headed arrow and click** to select the text box.

    b. In the Arrange group, **click Text Wrapping and select Square.**

    c. In the Arrange group, **click Align and select Align Right** to align the text box to the right side of the document.

Who We Are
Burke Properties is a full-service real estate brokerage firm. We provide a broad range of real estate services including residential and commercial sales and leasing. Jan Burke, the principal broker, has been personally involved in all phases of real estate for over 20 years. The brokers and associates of Burke Properties offer our clients a unique blend of specialties in the various markets within the area.

More sales in the last 10 years than any other area broker!

    d. **Save the document as *My Special Burke Graphics.docx* and close the document.**

ACTIVITY 5-2
Creating Pull Quotes

Data Files:

Newsletter Quotes.docx

Before You Begin:

From C:\084894Data\Creating Customized Graphic Elements, open Newsletter Quotes.docx.

Scenario:

You are working on the newsletter for your company. While explaining the history of the company, you wish to draw special attention to the fact that the company president has been involved in all phases of the business for over 20 years.

What You Do	How You Do It
1. **Insert a pull quote to highlight the history of the company.**	a. On the Insert tab, in the Text group, **click Text Box. Scroll down and select Cubicles Quote** to position the quote to the left of the document.
	b. **Scroll down** to view the text box.
	c. **Type** *Jan Burke, our President, has been personally involved in all phases of the real estate business for over 20 years.*
2. **Highlight the border of the pull quote.**	a. On the Text Box Tools Format contextual tab, in the Text Box Styles group, **click Shape Outline.**
	b. In the Shape Outline gallery, in the Standard Colors section, **select Dark Red, the first color from the left,** to highlight the border of the text box.

	c. **Save the document as** *My Newsletter Quotes.docx* **and close it.**

TOPIC B
Draw Shapes

In the previous topic, you inserted text boxes. Another type of graphic element you can insert to create a custom effect is a shape. In this topic, you will draw shapes to enhance documents.

Creating your own shapes is a practical way to add customized graphics to documents. Whether it's an arrow making a point, an attractive header for a paragraph, or a banner for your document's title, Word's drawing tools make it easy to create shapes accurately for the effect you want.

Shapes in Word

Definition:

A *shape* is a predefined figure that you can insert into a Word document to complement the text within it. You can insert a shape in a Word document using the Illustrations group on the Insert tab. After selecting a shape from the Shapes gallery, the mouse pointer changes to a crosshair. You can click and drag to draw the shape in the document. Shapes can be resized, reshaped, or rotated using the sizing handles that appear after drawing the shape. There are a variety of shapes such as lines, basic shapes, block arrows, and flowchart elements.

Example:

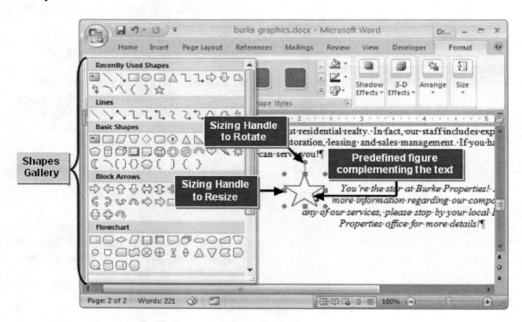

Types of Shapes

The Shapes gallery provides a wide range of shapes that you can add to documents. You can draw straight, curved, or free-form lines and connectors; squares, circles, cubes, arcs, and other common geometric shapes; block arrows with clearly defined borders; flowchart elements; callouts in various shapes; and a variety of stars and banners.

Drawing Options

There are different ways in which you can draw a shape.

- Hold down Shift as you drag to draw lines and arrows at 15-degree angles from the starting point.

- Hold down Ctrl as you draw lines or arrows to lengthen them from the starting point in both directions.

- Hold down Shift as you draw shapes to create proportionate shapes. For example, hold down Shift to draw a circle with an Oval tool or a square with the Rectangle tool.

The Drawing Canvas

Definition:

The *drawing canvas* is a container for other graphics that enables you to manipulate shapes as a group. The drawing canvas itself is a drawn object. It is most useful if you are creating a compound drawing consisting of several shapes because it enables you to move and resize all the elements of the drawing as a single unit. The Scale Drawing option, in the right-click menu of a drawing canvas, is used to resize the elements within it proportionately. The drawing canvas can be inserted in Word by selecting New Drawing Canvas from the Shapes gallery. It does not appear by default when you insert a shape into a document. You can resize and format the drawing canvas to create a decorative frame for the objects within it.

Example:

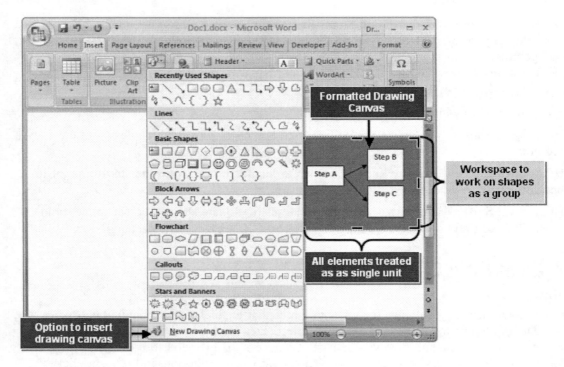

The Drawing Tools Format Contextual Tab

The Drawing Tools Format contextual tab contains various options within different groups that help format a shape. You can insert or change shapes; select styles, colors, and outlines; add shadows and 3-D effects; align, rotate, flip, or resize shapes; control text alignment and positioning; and group shapes to work on them as a unit.

How to Draw Shapes

Procedure Reference: Draw Shapes

To draw shapes in a document:

1. Place the insertion point where you want the shape to appear.
2. On the Insert tab, in the Illustrations group, click the Shapes button to display the Shapes gallery.
3. In the Shapes gallery, select the shape you want.
4. Drag to draw the shape.
5. If necessary, hold down Shift as you drag to create proportionate shapes.

Procedure Reference: Modify a Shape

To modify a shape:

1. Select the shape you want to modify.
2. To resize or rotate the shape manually, drag the sizing handles or rotate point.
3. To set a specific size, on the Drawing Tools Format contextual tab, in the Size group, type Height and Width values.

4. In the Shapes Styles group, select style, fill, outline, and shape options from the drop-down lists, or click the Dialog Box Launcher button and select the desired options in the Format AutoShape dialog box.

5. In the Shadow Effects group, select an option to set the shadow effect for the shape.
   - Click Shadow Effects and choose a shadow style.
   - Click the corresponding Nudge button to nudge the shadow towards a particular side.

6. Click 3-D Effects to select an option to set the 3-D effects for the shape.

7. In the Arrange group, set the position, text wrapping, alignment, and rotation for the shape.

Procedure Reference: Add Text to a Shape

To add text to a shape:

1. Select the shape to which you want to add the text.

2. Create a text box within the shape.
   - Right-click within the shape and choose Add Text.
   - Or, on the Format contextual tab, in the Insert Shapes group, click the Edit Text button.

3. Type the required text within the text box.

4. Click outside the text box to deselect it.

Procedure Reference: Insert a Drawing Canvas

To insert a drawing canvas:

1. Position the mouse pointer where you want the drawing canvas to be inserted.

2. On the Insert tab, in the Illustrations group, click the Shapes button.

3. In the Shapes gallery, select New Drawing Canvas to insert the drawing canvas.

4. If necessary, resize the drawing canvas by dragging its sizing handles to accommodate the required objects.

5. Insert any shapes or other objects you need into the drawing canvas.

6. To remove an object from the canvas, drag the object outside the canvas.

7. To delete an object from the canvas, select the object and press Delete.

ACTIVITY 5-3

Drawing a Shape

Data Files:

Burke Graphics.docx

Setup:

From C:\084894Data\Creating Customized Graphics Elements, open Burke Graphics.docx.

Scenario:

You are working on a two-page promotional flyer for Burke Properties. You have entered the necessary text for the flyer. You feel that an attractive heading would further enhance the flyer. An earlier flyer that you found used the Up Ribbon banner with the blue color. Moreover, one area of the document you want to call attention to is the final paragraph. To emphasize customer value, you decide to use a blue five-pointed star.

What You Do	How You Do It
1. Add a banner with the formatting you require.	a. In the Burke Graphics document, **place the insertion point before the second empty paragraph mark.**
	b. On the Insert tab, in the Illustrations group, **click Shapes** to display the Shapes gallery.
	c. In the Stars And Banners section, in the first row, **select the Up Ribbon (the fourth option from the right).**
	d. **Drag the mouse pointer from the second empty paragraph mark until just above the end of the word "firm"** so that it doesn't hide the "Who We Are" subheading.
	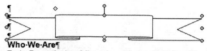
	e. In the Shape Styles group, **click the Shape Fill drop-down arrow** to display the color palette.
	f. In the Theme Colors section, in the first row, **select Accent 5, which is the second color from the right,** to apply it to the shape.
	g. In the Arrange group, **click the Align button and select Align Center** to center the banner.
2. Add the text BURKE PROPERTIES to the banner.	a. In the Insert Shapes group, **click the Edit Text button.**
	b. In the banner, **type *BURKE PROPERTIES***
	c. On the Home tab, in the Paragraph group, **click the Center button** to center the text within the banner.

3. Draw a star shape at the end of the document.

a. **Scroll to the bottom of the document.**

b. On the Insert tab, in the Illustrations group, **click Shapes** to display the Shapes gallery.

c. In the Stars And Banners section, **select 5-Point Star.**

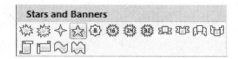

d. Before the text "You're the star", **drag** to draw a star with height and width measuring approximately 1 inch.

> **Finally...¶**
> Our·company·isn't·just·about·residential·realty.·In·fact,
> in:·historic·preservation,·restoration,·leasing·and·sales·r
> real·estate·need,·we·can·serve·you!¶
>
> *star·at·Burke·Properties!·For·more·infc*
> com ~any·of·our·services,·please·stop·by·your·lo
> *for·more·details!¶*

4. Format the star shape.

a. In the Shape Styles group, **click the Shape Fill drop-down arrow** to display the gallery.

b. In the Standard Colors section, **select the seventh color** to select light blue.

c. In the Shadow Effects group, **click Shadow Effects** to display the gallery.

d. In the Perspective Shadow section, in the first row, **select the first option** to apply a shadow effect to the star.

e. In the Arrange group, **click Text Wrapping and select In Line With Text** to wrap the shape in line with the text.

f. **Click at the end of the last paragraph** to deselect and view the shape.

g. **Save the document as *My Burke Graphics.docx* and close it.**

TOPIC C

Add WordArt and Other Special Effects to Text

In the first two topics, you inserted boxes and shapes that you can use to store text within a graphic. WordArt takes this idea one step further and enables you to turn the text itself into a graphic object. In this topic, you will add special effects to text using WordArt and drop caps.

Titles or section headings are the attention grabbers of any document and give a gist of what the reader should expect in the rest of the document. A simple way of highlighting titles or section headings is by making them bold or adding a color. Word allows you to go a step further and add special effects to blocks of text.

WordArt

Definition:

WordArt objects are decorative text elements you insert as graphic objects in a document. WordArt is a Microsoft Office System tool that provides you with a gallery of predefined WordArt effects, including shapes, colors, and shading for the WordArt object. After selecting a pre-defined WordArt effect, you need to provide the necessary text that will appear as the WordArt. The WordArt option is available in the Text group on the Insert tab. You can also size or format WordArt as you would any other graphic object.

Example:

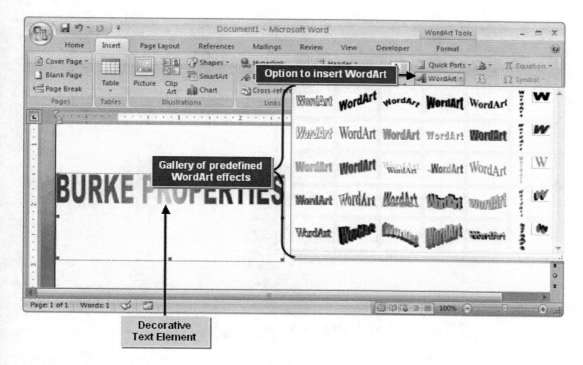

The WordArt Tools Format Contextual Tab

Once you insert WordArt, you can modify it by using the formatting options available in different groups on the WordArt Tools Format contextual tab. You can set text editing, spacing, and alignment options; style, fill color, outline color, and graphic shape; shadow and 3-D effects; and size, position, wrapping, alignment, and rotation.

Drop Caps

Definition:

A *drop cap* is a text effect in Word that creates a large capital letter at the beginning of a paragraph. You can create this effect by using the Drop Cap button in the Text group on the Insert tab. You can set advanced options for the drop cap in the Drop Cap dialog box, including font type, number of lines which the letter should drop, and the distance from the remaining text. There are two default Drop Cap styles, Dropped and In Margin, that can be used to extend the Drop Cap within the paragraph or in the margin, respectively.

Example:

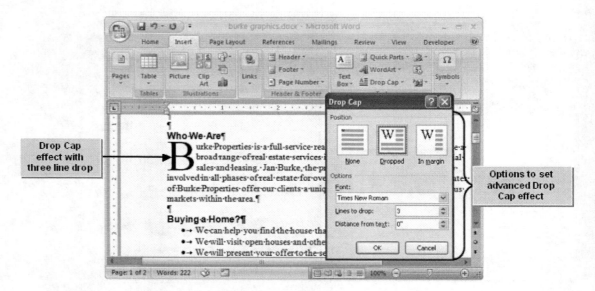

How to Add Special Effects to Text

Procedure Reference: Insert WordArt

To insert WordArt:

1. Place the insertion point where you want the WordArt to appear, or select existing text you want to convert to WordArt.

2. On the Insert tab, in the Text group, click WordArt and select a WordArt style from the WordArt gallery.

3. To modify the text, in the Edit WordArt Text dialog box, in the Text area, type the WordArt text.

4. To set basic text formatting, select a font and font size, and click Bold or Italics.

5. Click OK to insert the WordArt object.

6. To edit the WordArt text after it is inserted, on the WordArt Tools Format contextual tab, click Edit Text.

7. Format the WordArt object by selecting the appropriate options on the WordArt Tools Format contextual tab. In addition to the normal formatting options for graphic objects, you can control the amount of spacing for the text within the WordArt and kern the WordArt text.

Procedure Reference: Add a Drop Cap Effect

To add a Drop Cap effect:

1. Place the insertion point at the beginning of the paragraph to which you want the Drop Cap effect to be applied.

2. On the Insert tab, in the Text group, click Drop Cap.

3. Select Dropped or In Margin to place the letter within the paragraph or in the margin. Or you can select Drop Cap Options to set the font, number of lines to drop, and the distance from the main text.

ACTIVITY 5-4

Adding Special Effects to Text

Data Files:

Burke Word.docx

Setup:

From C:\084894Data\Creating Customized Graphics Elements, open Burke Word.docx

Scenario:

You want to create a prominent look for the "Burke Properties" title in the document. You don't think you can accomplish the effects you want just by using font formatting options. Additionally, you want the first paragraph to make an impact. So, you decide to work on the first letter of the paragraph.

What You Do	How You Do It
1. Set a WordArt style.	a. **Verify that the insertion point is placed before the first paragraph mark at the top of the page.**
	b. On the Insert tab, in the Text group, **click WordArt** to display the WordArt gallery.
	c. In the top row, **select WordArt Style 3,** which has the arched style.
	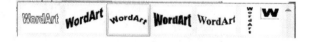
	d. In the Edit WordArt Text dialog box, in the Text text box, **type Burke Properties**
	e. **Click OK** to insert the WordArt object in the document.
	f. On the Home tab, in the Paragraph group, **click the Center button** to center the WordArt object.
2. Apply a blue color to the WordArt object.	a. On the WordArt Tools Format contextual tab, in the WordArt Styles group, **click the Shape Fill button** to display the color palette.

b. In the Theme Colors section, in the first row, **select Accent 5, which is the second color from the right,** to apply it to the WordArt object.

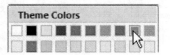

3. **Drop the first letter of the paragraph four lines.**

a. **Place the insertion point at the beginning of the paragraph that begins with the text "Burke Properties".**

b. On the Insert tab, in the Text group, **click Drop Cap** to display the Drop Cap menu.

c. **Choose Drop Cap Options** to display the Drop Cap dialog box.

d. In the Position section, **select Dropped** to drop the first letter in the paragraph.

e. In the Options section, from the Font drop-down list, **select the Tempus Sans ITC font style.**

f. In the Lines To Drop spin box, **select 4** to drop the letter four lines in the paragraph.

g. **Click OK** to apply the Drop Cap effect.

h. **Click after the text "Who We Are"** to deselect and view the Drop Cap effect.

Who We Are

Burke Properties is a full-ser broad range of real estate s sales and leasing. Jan Burk involved in all phases of re associates of Burke Properties offe various markets within the area.

i. **Save the document as *My Burke Word-.docx* and close it.**

TOPIC D
Create Complex Illustrations with SmartArt

You have created and modified various types of individual graphic elements such as shapes, lines, and text boxes. Common business diagrams, such as organization charts or Venn diagrams, combine a number of different simple graphic elements to create more complex structures. In this topic, you will use SmartArt to create complex illustrations.

It can be cumbersome to create an organization chart by drawing all the shapes, lines, and text boxes by hand. Word's dedicated diagramming tools help you build sharp, professional-looking business diagrams much more easily than you can with freehand drawing. All you have to do is specify the content and structure for the diagram and leave the drawing to Word.

SmartArt Graphics

Definition:

A *SmartArt graphic* is a preset image used to illustrate information in a document by showing a process, hierarchy, or other relationships between items. It is a combination of text, illustration, and color. Each SmartArt graphic, based on its design, maps the text outline and automatically resizes it for the best fit onto the graphic. The shape and text in a SmartArt graphic can be formatted.

Example:

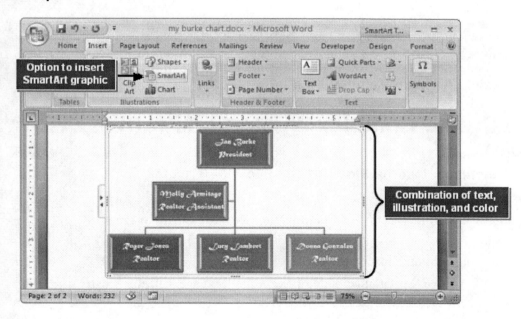

The Choose A SmartArt Graphic Dialog Box

The three panes in the Choose A SmartArt Graphic dialog box enable you to select, preview, and insert a SmartArt graphic. You can select a SmartArt graphic category, pick a layout within that category, and preview the layout as well as read a brief description of its purpose.

SmartArt Graphic Categories

There are various types of SmartArt graphics available to illustrate information.

Type	Used To Represent
List	Non-sequential or grouped blocks of information.
Process	A progression of events, or sequential steps.
Cycle	A continuing sequence of information in a circular flow.
Hierarchy	Hierarchical information such as an organizational chart.
Relation-ship	Any one of a number of diverse connections between tasks, events, or stages.
Matrix	The relationship of four quadrants to the whole.
Pyramid	Proportional or interconnected relationships.

SmartArt Tools

SmartArt Tools is a contextual feature of Word which is activated when a SmartArt graphic is inserted in a document. It constitutes two tabs which help in formatting and structuring a SmartArt graphic. The SmartArt Tools Format contextual tab is instrumental in enhancing the overall style and effect of the SmartArt graphic, whereas the SmartArt Tools Design contextual tab helps to format individual entities within a graphic.

How to Create Complex Illustrations with SmartArt

Procedure Reference: Insert a SmartArt Graphic

To insert a SmartArt graphic:

1. Place the insertion point where you would like to insert the SmartArt graphic.
2. Select the Insert tab.
3. In the Illustrations group, click SmartArt.
4. In the Choose A SmartArt Graphic dialog box, in the left pane, select a SmartArt graphic type.
5. In the center pane, select the desired layout.
6. After previewing the selected layout in the right pane, click OK to insert the selected layout in the document.
7. Add text to the graphic.
   - Use the text pane to insert text.
     a. Click the tab on the SmartArt object to open the text pane.

b. In the text pane, select each object and type the desired text.

c. To insert a new object, press Enter.

d. Close the text pane.

● Or, double-click the desired shape in the SmartArt graphic and enter the text.

8. Save and close the document.

Procedure Reference: Modify a SmartArt Graphic

To modify a SmartArt graphic:

1. Select the SmartArt graphic.

2. On the Ribbon, select the SmartArt Tools Design contextual tab.

3. In the Create Graphic group, select the options to add, move, and edit the text of a shape in the graphic.

   ● Click Add Shape to insert a new shape.

   ● If necessary, click Add Bullet to add a bulleted list to the shape.

   ● Click Right To Left to reverse the direction of a shape in the SmartArt graphic.

   ● Click Text Pane to display the text pane to edit the text.

4. In the Layouts group, click the More button and select a layout style for the graphic.

5. In the SmartArt Styles group, select an overall visual style and color scheme.

   ● Click the More button and select a style from the gallery.

   ● Click Change Colors and select a color scheme.

6. If necessary, in the Reset group, select Reset Graphic to remove all the formatting changes and restore the graphic to its original form.

7. On the Ribbon, select the SmartArt Tools Format contextual tab.

8. In the Shapes group, select the options to change the type and size of a shape in the graphic.

9. In the Shapes Styles group, select a style, fill color, outline color, and visual effect.

10. In the WordArt Styles group, select a WordArt style, fill color, outline, and text effect for the text within the shapes.

11. In the Arrange group, set the positioning, alignment, and text wrapping options.

12. In the Size group, set the height and width of the shape.

ACTIVITY 5-5

Creating a Complex Illustration

Data Files:

Burke Chart.docx

Before You Begin

From C:\084894Data\Creating Customized Graphics Elements, open Burke Chart.docx.

Scenario:

You would like to add some information to your document about the new client service staff that Burke Properties has added. However, you don't think a simple list of names will add much visual interest to the document. You decide to represent the list of names in a hierarchical manner. To make this representation match the rest of the document, you will use shades of blue.

Your completed chart will look similar to the following graphic:

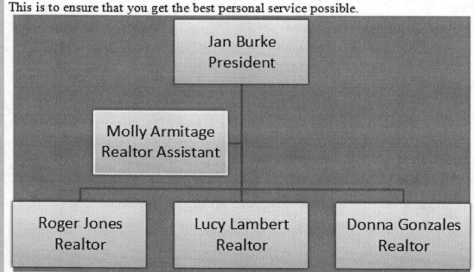

What You Do	How You Do It
1. Insert a basic organization chart.	a. Below the vertical scroll bar, **click the Next Page button** to move to the top of the second page of the document.
	b. On Page 2, **place the insertion point on the paragraph mark in the blank line after the first paragraph,** just above the word "Finally".
	c. On the Ribbon, **select the Insert tab.**
	d. In the Illustrations group, **click SmartArt.**
	e. In the Choose A SmartArt Graphic dialog box, in the left pane, **select Hierarchy.**
	f. In the center pane, in the first row, **select Organization Chart,** which is the first option.

	g. In the right pane, **read the description of the SmartArt graphic and click OK.**
2. Enter the organizational details.	a. **Click in the first shape at the top level, type *Jan Burke* and press Enter.**
	b. **Type *President***
	c. **Click in the shape in the second level, type *Molly Armitage* and press Enter.**
	d. **Type *Realtor Assistant***
	e. In the third level, in the first, second, and third organizational shapes, **type *Roger Jones Realtor, Lucy Lambert Realtor*, and *Donna Gonzales Realtor,*** respectively.

3.   Apply a style to the chart.

a.   On the SmartArt Tools Design contextual tab, in the SmartArt Styles group, **select the third style.**

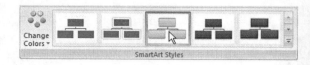

b.   **Click anywhere within the organizational chart, away from the shapes,** to select the entire organizational chart.

c.   **Select the SmartArt Tools Format contextual tab.**

d.   In the Shape Styles group, **click Shape Fill.**

e.   In the Standard Colors section, **select the seventh color from the left** to select light blue.

f.   **Click after the text "We're Growing"** to deselect the chart and view it.

g.   **Save the document as** *My Burke Chart.docx* **and close it.**

Lesson 5 Follow-up

In this lesson, you created customized graphic elements to use in your business documents. Word gives you the ability to create the specific graphic element you need to suit your document.

1. **Which illustrations will you normally use in your documents? Why?**

2. **How can you make your documents visually appealing and engaging?**

6 Inserting Content Using Quick Parts

Lesson Time: 40 minutes

Lesson Objectives:

In this lesson, you will insert content using Quick Parts.

You will:

- Insert building blocks.
- Create building blocks.
- Modify building blocks.
- Insert fields using Quick Parts.

Introduction

So far in this course, you have inserted a number of Word elements into your documents, including tables, text boxes, and various graphics. Word provides a simple way for you to insert many of these types of components from a gallery of stored objects. In this lesson, you will insert content into a document using Quick Parts.

You have seen the convenience of adding pre-built content blocks, such as standard headers and footers, from the various galleries available in Word. You have also seen the advantages of creating some of your own content when needed. Word 2007 offers you a tool that offers you the advantages of both. The Quick Parts tool not only gives you access to all the different galleries of content available by default in Word, it enables you to create and save your own content blocks, as well as to organize, manage, sort, and modify all standard document components from a central location.

TOPIC A
Insert Building Blocks

In this lesson, you will insert content into your document using Quick Parts. A common use of Quick Parts is to insert reusable content that is stored in predefined building blocks. In this topic, you will insert building blocks.

While documenting information, you might come across various instances where you need to repeat chunks of text time and again. Copying, pasting, and retyping frequently used information can be an arduous task. Word provides easy-to-access features to quickly insert reusable blocks of information in a document.

Building Blocks

Definition:

A *building block* is a preformatted piece of content that can be reused within or across Word documents. Building blocks can be built in or user defined. Built-in building blocks are available in the various galleries throughout Word. You can save any type of information, such as headers, footers, page numbers, cover pages, and text boxes as a user-defined building block, and add the block to the appropriate gallery. You can also resize and format a building block.

Example:

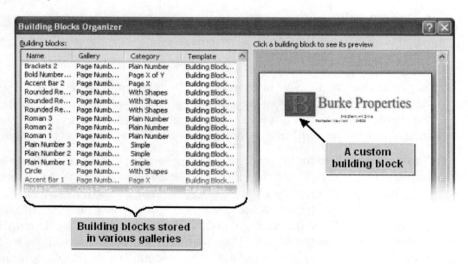

Quick Parts

Quick Parts is a tool in Word that is used to organize and insert all types of reusable content, including all of Word's pre-made building blocks, any user-created building blocks, and fields. The Quick Parts menu appears on the Text group on the Insert tab. The Quick Parts menu includes its own gallery where users can add custom content.

The Quick Parts menu has options to work with reusable elements of a document.

Quick Parts Menu Option	Used To
Quick Parts Gallery	Insert custom building blocks that the user has added to the Quick Parts gallery.
Document Property	Insert document properties such as author, company name, title, and so on.
Field	Insert placeholders for data that can be updated regularly.
Page Numbers	Insert page numbers in the document.
Building Blocks Organizer	Display the Building Blocks Organizer dialog box.
Get More On Office Online	Download building blocks from the Internet.
Save Selection to Quick Part Gallery	Save selected content as a building block, and add it to the Quick Parts gallery or any other Word gallery.

The Building Blocks Organizer Dialog Box

The Building Blocks Organizer dialog box is used to insert, organize, and modify reusable pieces of information.

Option	Used To
Building Blocks pane	Sort and view the building blocks based on the name, gallery, category, template, behavior, and description.
Click A Building Block To See Its Preview pane	Preview the selected building block.
Edit Properties button	Display the Modify Building Block dialog box and edit the properties of the building block.
Delete button	Delete a selected building block.
Insert button	Insert a selected building block.

The Building Blocks Pane

The Building Blocks pane in the Building Blocks Organizer dialog box displays a list of all available building blocks, both custom and predefined. The Building Blocks pane lists each building block with its details, such as the name, the gallery in which it appears, the category within the gallery, the template in which it is stored, its behavior, and a description. You can click the column headings to sort the building blocks by name, gallery, category, or template.

How to Insert Building Blocks

Procedure Reference: Insert a Building Block Using the Building Blocks Organizer

To insert a building block using the Building Blocks Organizer:

1. Place the insertion point in the document at the place you want the building block to appear.

2. On the Insert tab, in the Text group, click Quick Parts.

3. From the Quick Parts menu, select Building Blocks Organizer.

4. In the Building Blocks Organizer dialog box, click the Name, Gallery, Category, Template, Behavior, or Description tab to sort building blocks.

5. In the Building Blocks pane, select a building block.

6. In the Click A Building Block To See Its Preview pane, preview the selected building block.

7. Click Insert to insert the building block.

ACTIVITY 6-1

Inserting Building Blocks

Data Files:

Annual Report.docx

Before You Begin:

From C:\084894Data\Inserting Content Using Quick Parts, open Annual Report.docx.

Scenario:

You have almost finished preparing the Annual Report for your company. You need to number the pages in your document. You also need to insert some supporting information about the history of the company in the document. You would like to quickly find a sidebar and a page numbering format that you have used in previous cases.

What You Do	How You Do It
1. **Add sidebars to insert additional information in the document.**	a. **Scroll down to the second page of the document.**
	b. **Place the insertion point at the beginning of the text "Financial".**
	c. On the Insert tab, in the Text group, **click Quick Parts and choose Building Blocks Organizer.**
	d. The blocks are sorted by gallery. **Click the Name column heading** to sort the blocks by their names.
	e. In the Building Blocks Organizer dialog box, **scroll down and select the Puzzle Sidebar in the Text Boxes gallery, and click Insert** to display the sidebar outline on the right side of the page.
	f. **Scroll down** to view the text box in the sidebar.
	g. **Type** *Founded in 1946 by John Burke, Burke Properties is a full-service real estate agency.*

2. **Number the pages using the Large Color 1 building block.**

    a. On the Insert tab, in the Text group, **click Quick Parts and choose Building Blocks Organizer.**

    b. In the Building Blocks Organizer dialog box, **scroll down and select the Large Color 1 building block from the Page Number gallery.**

    c. **Click Insert** to insert page numbers in the document.

    d. **Click the Office button and choose Print→Print Preview.**

    e. **Scroll down to verify that all the pages are numbered.**

    f. Notice the sidebar placement and the page numbering in the preview and **close Print Preview.**

    g. **Save the document as *My Annual Report.docx***

TOPIC B
Create Building Blocks

In the previous topic, you inserted predefined building blocks. If you want to store custom combinations of text and graphics for reuse, you can create your own building blocks. In this topic, you will create building blocks.

While creating documents, you might come across various instances where you repeat blocks of information. Most official documents have standard ways of presenting content and have some style requirements. Some of them may also have standard text that is repeated within the pages of a document or across similar documents. Word lets you insert such standard information blocks into documents quickly.

The Create New Building Block Dialog Box

The Create New Building Block dialog box is used to specify the properties of a custom building block. You can use the Create New Building Block dialog box to specify the name, gallery, category, description, and template for the building block. You can also set options to insert the building block in a separate page, as a separate paragraph, or with other insertion settings. If you save the building block in the Quick Parts gallery, it will be available from the Quick Parts drop-down list for quick insertion.

How to Create Building Blocks

Procedure Reference: Create a Custom Building Block

To create a custom building block:

1. In the document, select the text or graphic you want to save as a building block.
2. On the Insert tab, in the Text group, click Quick Parts.
3. From the Quick Parts menu, choose Save Selection To Quick Part Gallery to launch the Create New Building Block dialog box.
4. In the Create New Building Block dialog box, in the Name text box, type a name for the building block.
5. From the Gallery drop-down list, select a gallery for the building block.
   - Select a built-in gallery to save the building block in an existing gallery.
   - Select a custom option to save the building block in a newly created custom gallery.
6. From the Category drop-down list, select a category for the building block.
   - Select General to save the building block in the general section of the gallery.
   - Select Built-In to save the building block in the built-in section of the gallery.
   - Select Create New Category, type a name for the category, and click OK.
7. If necessary, in the Description text box, type a description for the building block.
8. From the Save In drop-down list, select the Building Blocks.dotx template or the Normal.dotm global template.

9. From the Options drop-down list, select a behavior setting for the building block.

   ● Select Insert Content In Its Own Page to insert the building block on a separate page with page breaks before and after it.

   ● Select Insert In Its Own Paragraph to insert the building block as a separate paragraph.

   ● Select Insert Content Only for default insert settings.

10. Click OK to create a new building block.

11. Insert the building block into documents as needed.

ACTIVITY 6-2
Creating a Building Block

Data Files:

Burke Properties.docx

Before You Begin:

My Annual Report is open.

From C:\084894Data\Inserting Content Using Quick Parts, open Burke Properties.docx.

Scenario:

You find it necessary to add company information as standard details in all your documents. Instead of adding and formatting these details each time, you decide to save them as reusable bits of content. Also, saving this information in a readily accessible repository containing similar content within the application itself seems to be a good idea. You can use the standard information immediately in your document.

What You Do	How You Do It
1. **Display the Create New Building Block dialog box.**	a. In the Burke Properties document, **select the logo, title, and address of Burke Properties, including the last two paragraph marks.**
	b. On the Insert tab, in the Text group, **click Quick Parts.**
	c. From the Quick Parts menu, **choose Save Selection To Quick Part Gallery** to display the Create New Building Block dialog box.

2. **Store the building block in the Quick Parts gallery.**

   a. In the Create New Building Block dialog box, in the Name text box, **type *Burke Properties***

   b. In the Gallery text box, **verify that Quick Parts is selected.**

   c. From the Category drop-down list, **select Create New Category.**

   d. In the Create New Category dialog box, in the Name text box, **type *Document Masthead* and click OK.**

   e. **Click OK** to save the building block.

   f. **Close the Burke Properties document without saving any changes.**

3. **Insert the custom masthead into the Annual Report document.**

   a. **Verify that the cursor is at the top of Annual Report.**

   b. On the Insert tab, in the Text group, **click Quick Parts.**

   c. The custom masthead appears in the Quick Parts gallery. **Click the custom masthead** to insert it.

   d. **Save the document.**

TOPIC C
Modify Building Blocks

You have now created and inserted building blocks in your document. You may want to edit the properties or content of a building block. In this topic, you will modify building blocks.

There might be a built-in building block that is close to what you are looking for. Also, this building block may not be appropriately located for you to find it easily. You can make this building block a starting point for your customization. With a few minor modifications, it will become better suited for your requirements. Modifying a building block can save the time that you would probably spend creating it from the beginning.

Building Block Modification Options

You can modify the content of a custom or built-in building block by creating a new building block with the same name as an existing building block. You can also use the Modify Building Block dialog box to edit the properties of a building block, such as its name, gallery, category, and description.

How to Modify Building Blocks

Procedure Reference: Customize a Building Block

To customize a building block:

1. On the Insert tab, in the Text group, click Quick Parts and choose Building Blocks Organizer.

2. In the Building Blocks Organizer dialog box, select a building block and insert it in the document.

3. Customize the building block using the respective contextual tabs.

4. On the Insert tab, in the Text group, click Quick Parts and choose Save Selection To Quick Part Gallery to save the building block.

5. Save the building block with the same name to overwrite the existing building block, or with a new name to create a new building block.

6. If you are overwriting an existing building block, click Yes when prompted to redefine the building block.

Procedure Reference: Edit the Properties of a Building Block

To edit the properties of a building block:

1. On the Insert tab, in the Text group, click Quick Parts and choose Building Blocks Organizer.

2. In the Building Blocks Organizer dialog box, select a building block and click Edit Properties.

3. In the Modify Building Block dialog box, specify the desired name, gallery, category, description, template, and any building block options.

4. Click OK to modify the properties of the building block.

5. In the Microsoft Office Word message box, click Yes to redefine the building block entry.

ACTIVITY 6-3

Modifying a Building Block

Before You Begin:

My Annual Report.docx is open.

Scenario:

You have created and saved a custom masthead as a building block, but you realize the ZIP Code is missing from the address. You need to modify the building block so that it will be correct the next time you insert it. You also feel that the name you originally gave the building block was too general, so you want to make it more specific.

What You Do	How You Do It
1. **Customize the custom building block for the Burke Properties masthead.**	a. At the top of the document, **click after the words "New York".**
	b. **Press Tab and type** *14623*
	c. **Select the entire masthead, including the text and the logo.**
	d. On the Insert tab, in the Text group, **click Quick Parts and choose Save Selection To Quick Part Gallery.**
	e. In the Name text box, **type** *Burke Properties*
	f. In the Gallery text box, **verify that Quick Parts is selected.**
	g. From the Category drop-down list, **select Document Masthead.**
	h. **Click OK.**
	i. In the Microsoft Office Word message box, **click Yes** to redefine the building block entry.
	j. **Click Quick Parts** to verify that the updated masthead appears in the gallery, and then **click the document** to close the menu.

2. **Rename the Burke Properties building block.**

a. On the Insert tab, in the Text group, **click Quick Parts and choose Building Blocks Organizer.**

b. **Click the Gallery column heading** to sort the list by gallery.

c. **Scroll down to the Quick Parts section of the list, select the Burke Properties building block, and click Edit Properties.**

d. In the Modify Building Block dialog box, in the Name text box, **type *Burke Masthead***

e. **Click OK** to modify the properties of the building block.

f. In the Microsoft Office Word message box, **click Yes** to redefine the building block entry.

g. **Click Close.**

h. **Save the document.**

TOPIC D
Insert Fields Using Quick Parts

In the first three topics of this lesson, you used Quick Parts to insert and manage building block content. You can also use Quick Parts to insert Word fields into documents. In this topic, you will insert fields using Quick Parts.

There might be instances when you have to insert document content that needs to be upgraded at regular intervals of time. Inserting fields is one way of doing this. Word gives you options to quickly insert fields in a document and update them when the need arises.

Fields

Definition:

A *field* is a small set of instructions inserted into a Word document that dynamically displays specific pieces of variable information, such as the current date, time, or page number. *Field codes* are the underlying programming instructions that determine the resulting field value. By default, Word normally displays the results of the field in the document, but you can choose to display the field codes instead. As information or conditions change, the results of the field will change to reflect the new information.

Example:

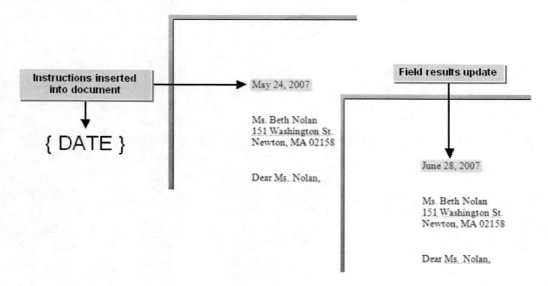

Field Categories

There are various categories of fields, each containing a group of fields with common features. These include:

- Date And Time fields.
- Document Automation fields, for controlling macros, evaluating conditional arguments, and so on.
- Document Information fields to store items such as the author's name, number of pages, or number of words.
- Equations And Formulas fields.
- Index And Tables fields.
- Links And References fields, for Autotext entries, footnotes, quotes, and other reference information.
- Mail Merge fields for generating form letters.
- Numbering fields for sections, page numbers, and other document components.
- User Information fields for the user's address, initials, and name.

Field Code Syntax

Specific field codes vary, but they all follow the same basic syntax.

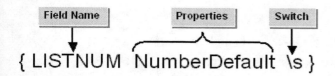

Figure 6-1: The basic syntax of a field code.

Syntax Element	Description
Field name	The basic function the field performs.
Properties	Any information that is required for the field to return a result. If there are spaces in an argument, it is enclosed in quotes.
Switches	Any number of variables that can be used with the field to control the field results. Available switches vary from field to field.

 One case in which you might use field codes to insert text instead of typing the text (such as an author's name) is when you are including the field in a macro. For example, you might create a macro that inserts several different fields of information about a document in a document footer. Each user who runs the macro will get customized text.

Available Word Fields

To see a list of the fields available in Word and the individual syntax for each field, on the Insert tab, in the Text group, click Quick Parts and choose Field. Individual descriptions and help for each field are available in the Microsoft Office Word Help system.

The Field Dialog Box

The Field dialog box, available from the Quick Parts menu, provides various options to work with fields in a document.

Field Dialog Box Option	Allows You To
Please Choose A Field section	• Select a field category such as date and time, document information, or equations and formulas from the Categories drop-down list. • Select the desired field from the Field Names list.
Field Properties section	Modify properties that are specific to a particular field.
Field Options section	Set advanced field options that are unique to the respective fields.
Field Codes button or Hide Codes button	Display or hide the field codes in the dialog box.
Preserve Formatting During Updates check box	Retain the formatting even after a field's content is updated.

How to Insert Fields Using Quick Parts

Procedure Reference: Insert a Field

To insert a field:

1. On the Insert tab, in the Text group, click Quick Parts and choose Field.
2. In the Field dialog box, in the Please Choose A Field section, from the Categories drop-down list, select a category.
   a. In the Field Names list box, select a field.
   b. In the Field Properties section, modify the options or format the selected field, as desired.
3. Click OK to insert the selected field in the document.
4. To toggle the display between the field results and the field codes, press Alt+F9.

Procedure Reference: Edit a Field

To edit a field:

1. Right-click within the field to display the menu.
2. From the menu options, select Edit Field to display the Field dialog box.
3. In the Field dialog box, modify the options or format the selected field, as desired.
4. Click OK to insert the edited field in the document.

ACTIVITY 6-4
Inserting a Field

Data Files:

Annual Report Modified.docx

Before You Begin:

My Annual Report.docx is open.

Scenario:

Your company's Annual Report is ready for manager review. However, your manager is on leave and can verify the report only after the weekend. So, you need to ensure that the date in the document is updated accordingly and the date format is appropriate for the document.

What You Do	How You Do It
1. **Insert the date field at the top of the document.**	a. At the top of the document, **click next to the paragraph mark on the empty line before the text "Fiscal Year and Accomplishments".**
	b. On the Insert tab, in the Text group, **click Quick Parts and choose Field.**
	c. In the Field dialog box, in the Please Choose A Field section, from the Categories drop-down list, **select Date and Time.**
	d. In the Field Names list box, **select Date** to insert the present date field.
	e. In the Field Properties section, in the Date Formats list box, **select the second option and click OK** to insert the date field in the document.

Monday, May 21, 2007

Fiscal·Year·and·Accomplishments¶

This·fiscal·year·was·truly·a·foundation-building·year·for·Burke·Properties,·Inc.·Fueled·by·a·continued·strong·economy·and·robust·commercial·real·estate·markets,·we·significantly·increased·our·revenues·and·earnings,·strengthened·our·balance·sheet,·and·put·in·place·a·solid·platform·from·which·we·can·now·aggressively·implement·our·long-term·growth·strategy.·Among·our·fiscal·accomplishments,·Burke·Properties.¶

2. You do not need the day of the week to display. **Edit the field to display the date in a numeric format.**

a. **Right-click the field and choose Edit Field.**

b. In the Field dialog box, in the Field Properties section, in the Date Formats list box, **select the third option and click OK** to display the date in the numeric format.

c. **Save and close the document.**

Lesson 6 Follow-up

In this lesson, you inserted content using Quick Parts. By using the Quick Parts tool to manage all of Word's reusable content, you can access content and manage it all in a centralized location, as well as store your own custom content for easy reuse.

1. **What kind of content will you reuse as building blocks in your documents?**

2. **What are the advantages of using the Building Blocks Organizer rather than inserting content from the various Word galleries?**

7 | Controlling Text Flow

Lesson Time: 45 minutes

Lesson Objectives:

In this lesson, you will control text flow.

You will:

- Control paragraph flow.
- Insert section breaks.
- Insert columns.
- Link text boxes to control text flow.

Introduction

You have created and modified various separate document elements. Now, it is time to take a step back and consider the flow of content in the document. In this lesson, you will control text flow in your Word documents.

Documents don't always contain simple margin-to-margin text. Sometimes, you need to break up the text or make it flow differently on the page. For example, think of a departmental newsletter that you want lay out in two columns with a banner headline spanning the columns. You might have two different stories that both start on page 1 and then continue on other pages of the document. These are the kinds of effects you can achieve by modifying a document's text flow.

TOPIC A
Control Paragraph Flow

In this lesson, you will control text flow in Word documents. Because most document content is stored in paragraph form, a good place to start is by controlling text flow within and between paragraphs. In this topic, you will control paragraph flow.

As you customize your document, you may find that continuous paragraphs are not on the same page. If your document contains graphics, you may find that the picture has caused a paragraph to be pushed all the way to the last page of the document. It's easy to fix these little layout problems by setting options to control paragraph flow.

Paragraph Flow Options

The Line And Page Breaks tab in the Paragraph dialog box displays several options to control paragraph flow.

Paragraph Flow Option	Effect When Enabled
Widow/Orphan Control	Prevents *widows* (a single line at the top of a page) and *orphans* (a single line at the bottom of a page). Widow/Orphan Control is on by default.
Keep With Next	Ensures that the current paragraph will always appear on the same page as the paragraph that follows it. This option is useful for a heading or title paragraph that leads into a paragraph of text.
Keep Lines Together	Prevents selected lines from splitting across a page break.
Page Break Before	Ensures that the paragraph will always be first on a page.

How to Control Paragraph Flow
Procedure Reference: Control Paragraph Flow

To control paragraph flow:

1. Place the insertion point in the desired paragraph or select multiple paragraphs.
2. Display the Paragraph dialog box:
   - On the Home tab, in the Paragraph group, click the Paragraph Dialog Box Launcher button.
   - Or, right-click the selection and choose Paragraph.
3. Select the Line And Page Breaks tab.
4. On the Line And Page Breaks tab, in the Pagination section, check the appropriate check boxes to specify the desired paragraph flow options.
5. Verify the results of the settings in a Preview box and click OK to apply them to the document.

ACTIVITY 7-1

Controlling Paragraph Flow

Data Files:

Stockholder Review.docx

Before You Begin:

From C:\084894Data\Controlling Text Flow, open Stockholder Review.docx.

Scenario:

You're preparing some text to include in the Burke Properties Annual Report. After drafting the text and inserting the graphics, you proofread the document to avoid issues related to formatting and layout. You notice that the pictures in the document are getting printed on pages that do not contain the paragraphs that introduce them.

What You Do	How You Do It
1. Set the paragraph flow options so that the introductory paragraph stays with Figure 1.	a. In the Stockholder Review document, **scroll to the bottom of the first page.**
	b. **Click inside the paragraph that starts with "Figure 1 shows".**
	c. On the Home tab, in the Paragraph group, **click the Paragraph Dialog Box Launcher button.**
	d. In the Paragraph dialog box, **select the Line And Page Breaks tab.**
	e. On the Line And Page Breaks tab, in the Pagination section, **verify that Widow/ Orphan Control is checked and check the Keep With Next check box.**

Pagination
- ☑ Widow/Orphan control
- ☑ Keep with next

	f. **Click OK** to move the paragraph to page 2, along with the figure.
	g. **Scroll down** to view the paragraph along with the graphic.

2. **Set the paragraph flow options so that the last topic appears on a separate page.**

a. At the bottom of the vertical scroll bar, **click the Next Page button until page 4 of the document is displayed.**

b. At the end of the page, **click just after the heading "OUTLOOK".**

c. On the Home tab, in the Paragraph group, **click the Paragraph Dialog Box Launcher button.**

d. In the Paragraph dialog box, on the Line And Page Breaks tab, in the Pagination section, **check the Page Break Before check box and click OK.**

e. **Scroll down** to view the headings on the next page.

f. **Save the document as *My Stockholder Review.docx* and close it.**

TOPIC B

Insert Section Breaks

In the previous topic, you controlled flow of text between existing paragraphs in a document. If you need to control flow settings for document divisions that are larger than a paragraph, you will need to divide the document into sections. In this topic, you will insert section breaks to split a document into different sections.

You may want to apply different page layout options to different parts of the same document. A single page may need different margin widths on different sections. Perhaps some pages need to print in landscape orientation while others will require portrait orientation. Section breaks let you achieve all these effects.

Sections and Section Breaks

Definition:

A *document section* is a portion of a document that can have page layout options set independently from other portions of the document. Page layout formatting that would normally apply to the entire document, such as headers and footers, page numbering, and page orientation, can be applied independently in each section. One section of a document is separated from the other with a *section break*. There are no automatic section breaks; you must insert them manually. You can view the sections in the Draft and Outline document views.

Example:

Types of Section Breaks

There are four types of section breaks.

Section Break Type	Description
Next Page	Starts the section on the next page. This lets you set different print options for the section such as paper source, size, type, and page orientation.
Continuous	Starts the section on the same page. This lets you set different margins for the sections on the same page.
Even Page	Starts the section on the next even-numbered page. The odd page in between becomes a blank page. Print Preview displays this blank page.
Odd Page	Starts the section on the next odd-numbered page. The even page in between becomes a blank page. Print Preview displays this blank page.

How to Insert Section Breaks

Procedure Reference: Insert or Delete a Section Break

To insert or delete a section break:

1. If necessary, on the Home tab, in the Paragraph group, click the Show/Hide button to display the paragraph formatting marks.
2. Place the insertion point on the paragraph mark just after the point where you need to insert a section break.
3. On the Page Layout tab, in the Page Setup group, click Breaks.
4. In the Breaks gallery, in the Section Breaks section, select the desired section break type.
5. To delete a section break, place the cursor on the section break that you wish to remove and press Delete to delete it. When a section break is deleted, the text becomes a part of the next section and thus takes on the formatting of that section.

Procedure Reference: Set Section Layout Options

To set layout options for a section of a document:

1. Place your insertion point in the section you want to modify.
2. On the Page Layout tab, in the Page Setup group, use the options to set the margins, orientation, paper size, and other page setup options for the section.
3. On the Insert tab, in the Header & Footer group, use the options to configure the header and footer for the section.
4. By default, a section inherits its header and footer from the previous section. To set an individualized header or footer for a given section, activate the header or footer for that section, and on the Header & Footer Tools Design tab, in the Navigation section, click Link To Previous. Click the button again if you want to restore the link.

ACTIVITY 7-2
Formatting a Document Section

Data Files:

Newsletter.docx

Before You Begin

From C:\084894Data\Controlling Text Flow, open Newsletter.docx.

Scenario:

You have created a newsletter for Burke Properties, Inc. The newsletter has a table with publication information, a blue-shaded masthead with the heading and subheading, and body text. As you review the newsletter, you find that the heading in the masthead is wrapping onto a second line. It would look better if there was room for this part of the heading to print on a single line. You also need trademark information to print on the first page of the document.

What You Do	**How You Do It**
1. Insert section breaks before and after the masthead.	a. At the top of the document, **place the insertion point before the paragraph mark immediately above the blue-shaded box of text.** (This is the second empty paragraph mark after the "Volume A" table.)
	b. On the Page Layout tab, in the Page Setup group, **click Breaks.**
	c. In the Section Breaks section, **select Continuous.**

	d. **Place the insertion point before the empty paragraph mark immediately above the text "About Us".**
	e. **Insert a Continuous section break.**

2. Increase the width of the text area to fit the masthead on a single line.

a. Position the insertion point anywhere between the two section breaks.

b. In the Page Setup group, **click the Dialog Box Launcher button** to open the Page Setup dialog box.

c. On the Margins tab, **change the Left and Right margins to 1 inch.**

d. In the Apply To drop-down list, **verify that This Section is selected and click OK.**

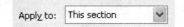

3. Insert the trademark information in the first section header.

a. Double-click the top margin of the first page of the document to open the Section 1 header.

b. **Type *Published by Burke Properties***

c. On the Insert tab, in the Symbols group, **click Symbol and select the trademark sign.**

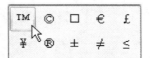

4. Unlink the remaining section headers.

a. On the Header & Footer Tools Design tab, in the Navigation group, **click Next Section.**

b. The header information appears in this section. The "Same As Previous" indicator shows that the section header is linked to the previous section header. On the Header & Footer Tools Design tab, in the Navigation group, **click Link To Previous.**

c. **Select and delete the text in the current section's header.**

d. In the Navigation group, **click Previous Section** to verify that the first section header is unchanged.

e. In the Close group, **click Close Header & Footer.**

5. **Preview the section header.**

    a. **Click the Office button and choose Print→Print Preview.**

    b. In the Zoom group, **click Two Pages.**

    c. The header appears on the first page only. **Click Close Print Preview.**

    d. **Save the document as** *My Newsletter.docx*

TOPIC C
Insert Columns

You have inserted header and footer information for a section. Applying section breaks is a common layout choice for many documents. However, another common option is to format the text so that it flows into multiple columns on a page. In this topic, you will insert columns into Word documents.

Imagine an article in a newspaper with pages and pages of text without any formatting. Readers would find it difficult to read through the information and would not pay attention to it no matter how interesting or informative the content is. Text formatting in columns can be easy on the eyes because there is more white space on the page.

Text Columns

Definition:

Text columns are layout options that organize and present text as columns on a page. In text columns, the text flows from one column to the next only after the space in the first column is filled. Also, as the text flows to the next page, it will start in the first column on the left-most part of the page. The columns can be customized by reducing the size or spacing between them. This layout can be applied to a particular section, from a selected point onward, or to the whole document. You can insert column breaks to force text after a break to wrap to the next column.

Example:

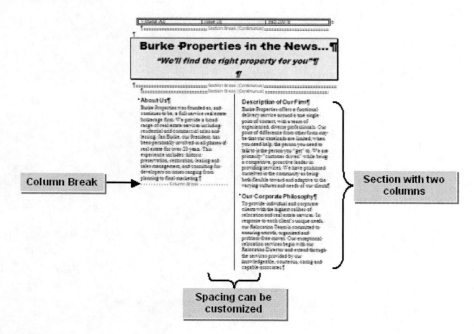

Text Column Options

You can use the Columns gallery to split the text into a maximum of three columns. It also provides options to either enlarge the first column or the second column in a two-column format.

The More Columns option in the gallery opens the Columns dialog box, where you can set a specific number of columns and customize column appearance.

Option	*Description*
Presets	Displays predefined column formats from which you can select the desired format.
Number Of Columns	Allows you to set the desired number of columns. A maximum of 13 columns can be set using the Number Of Columns text box.
Line Between	Allows you to display a vertical line between the columns.
Width And Spacing	Allows you to set dimensions for the columns' width and spacing. The Equal Column Width check box maintains an equal width among the columns.
Preview	Allows you to preview the chosen column format.
Apply To	Allows you to choose whether columns are to be applied to a particular section, from the selected point onward, or to the whole document.
Start New Column	Allows you to move the text following the insertion point to the top of the next column.

Paragraph Flow Settings in Columns

Paragraph flow settings, such as widow and orphan control, work across column breaks just as they work across page breaks.

How to Insert Columns

Procedure Reference: Insert Columns Using the Columns Gallery

To insert columns using the Columns gallery:

1. Place the insertion point where you want the new columns to start.
2. On the Page Layout tab, in the Page Setup group, click Columns.
3. In the Columns gallery, select a preset column format.

Procedure Reference: Insert and Format Columns Using the Columns Dialog Box

To insert and format columns using the Columns dialog box:

1. Place the insertion point where you want the new columns to start, or inside existing columns you want to format.
2. On the Page Layout tab, in the Page Setup group, click Columns and select More Columns.
3. Set the desired number of columns.
    *   Select an existing column format with the desired number of columns.
    *   Or, in the Number Of Columns text box, type the number of columns.

4. In the Columns dialog box, specify the desired width and spacing.

- Type specific Width and Spacing values for each individual column.

- Or, check Equal Column Width for balanced columns.

5. If necessary, check the Line Between check box to draw a vertical line between columns.

6. From the Apply To drop-down list, select an option to specify where you need to apply columns.

- Select Whole Document to apply columns to the entire document.

- Select This Section to apply columns to the current section of the document.

- Select This Point Forward to start the new section of columns after the section break, and, if necessary, check the Start New Column check box to move the text following the insertion point to the top of the next column.

7. Click OK.

Procedure Reference: Insert Column Breaks

To insert column breaks:

1. Place the insertion point just before the text you want to wrap to the next column.

2. In the Page Setup group, click Breaks and select Column.

ACTIVITY 7-3
Inserting Columns

Before You Begin

My Newsletter.docx is open

Scenario:

After reviewing several sample publications from other firms, you realize that most of them use a two-column format. You are wary of using columns because of the paragraph flow problems they create, but you also like the way columns help in presenting information.

What You Do	How You Do It
1. **Create a two-column layout with a separator line for the remaining portion of the document after the masthead.**	a. **Place the insertion point at the beginning of the text "About Us".**
	b. On the Page Layout tab, in the Page Setup group, **click Columns and select More Columns** to display the Columns dialog box.
	c. In the Columns dialog box, in the Presets section, **select Two** to insert a two-column layout.
	d. **Verify that the Line Between check box is checked** to display a line between the two columns.
	☑ Line between
	e. From the Apply To drop-down list, **select This Point Forward** to insert a section break before starting the new section of columns.
	f. **Click OK** to save the settings.

2. **Insert a column break.**

   a. **Scroll to the bottom of page 3.**

   b. The "Our New Web Site" subtitle is separated from the following paragraph. **Place the insertion point at the beginning of the "Our New Web Site" subtitle.**

   c. In the Page Setup group, **click Breaks.**

   d. In the Page Breaks section of the gallery, **select Column** to wrap the text to the next column.

   e. **Preview the document.**

   f. **Save the document and close it.**

TOPIC D

Link Text Boxes to Control Text Flow

In the previous topic, you controlled text flow by inserting columns. You can further achieve text-flow effects by linking the content of one text box to another. In this topic, you will link text boxes.

Columns in Word are in a newsletter style, which means the text flows continuously from one column to another. If you need to start an article on page 1 of a newsletter and continue it on page 3, simple newsletter style columns will not do. For layout effects like this, you need linked text boxes. Linking text boxes in documents like newsletters and reports applies a professional look to your document.

Linked Text Boxes

Definition:

Linked text boxes are two or more text boxes that are connected so that text that overflows the first box automatically appears in subsequent boxes. You can use linked text boxes to control where different sections of a continuous stream of text will appear within a document, as well as the sequence of text flow. Use the Create Link button to link each individual box to its predecessor in the chain. Use the Break Link button to unlink any box from the chain and delete the text in the box.

Example:

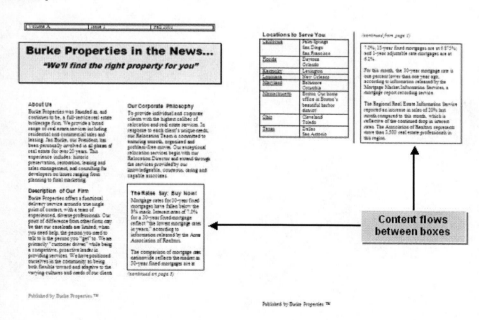

How to Link Text Boxes

Procedure Reference: Link Text Boxes

To link text boxes:

1. On the Microsoft Office status bar, select Print Layout view.
2. Insert the text boxes that you want to link at the desired locations in your document.
3. Click the border of the first text box to select it.
4. Enter text in the first text box.
5. Display the Format contextual tab.
6. In the Text group, click the Create Link button.
7. Click in the second text box to link the first text box to it.
8. If necessary, repeat the same process to link more text boxes.
9. If necessary, add text to the boxes after linking them.
10. Adjust the size, shape, and appearance of the text boxes, as necessary.
11. If necessary, select the text box and click the Break Link button to remove a text box from the linked chain, or press Esc to cancel the link.

ACTIVITY 7-4

Linking Text Boxes

Data Files:

Newsletter Box.docx, Rates Text.docx

Before You Begin

1. From C:\084894Data\Controlling Text Flow, open Rates Text.docx.
2. From C:\084894Data\Controlling Text Flow, open Newsletter Box.docx.

Scenario:

You are working on a newsletter for Burke Properties, Inc. Most of the content of the newsletter has been laid out and formatted in columns. The managing broker for your office has provided you with a separate document that contains the text for a fairly lengthy article on mortgage rates. You know this information will be of interest to your clients and you want to feature the article prominently, without taking up too much space on page 1.

What You Do	How You Do It
1. Copy the article text from the Rates Text document and paste it into the Newsletter Box document.	a. In the Newsletter Box document, **press Page Down** to view the first text box at the bottom of the second column on page 1.

(continued on page 3)

b. **Switch to Rates Text.docx.**

c. On the Home tab, in the Editing group, **click Select and select Select All.**

d. In the Clipboard group, **click the Copy button.**

e. **Close the Rates Text document.**

f. In the Newsletter Box document, **click in the text box on page 1.**

g. On the Home tab, in the Clipboard group, **click Paste** to insert the text into the text box. The text overflows the text box.

The Rates Say: Buy Now!

Mortgage rates for 30-year fixed mortgages have fallen below the 8% mark. Interest rates of 7.0% for a 30-year fixed mortgage reflect "the lowest mortgage rates in years," according to information released by the Acme Association of Realtors.

The comparison of mortgage rates nationwide reflects the market as 30-year fixed mortgages are at 7.0%. 15-year fixed mortgages

2. **Draw a text box to let the article flow to page 3.**

a. **Press Page Down three times** to move to the last page.

b. At the top of the second column on page 3, **place the insertion point before the paragraph mark below the text "Continued From Page 1".**

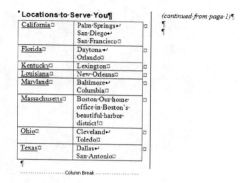

c. On the Ribbon, **select the Insert tab.**

d. In the Text group, **click Text Box and select Draw Text Box.**

e. **Click and drag** to draw a text box that is approximately equal in size to the table in the adjacent column.

3.   Link the text boxes.

a.   **Press Page Up three times** to move to the text box on page 1.

b.   **In the text box on page 1, click at the beginning of the text "The Rates Say: Buy Now!"** to select it.

c.   **Select the Text Box Tools Format contextual tab.**

d.   In the Text group, **click the Create Link button.**

e.   **Move the mouse pointer in the text area** to verify that the mouse pointer resembles a full pitcher. 🏺

f.   **Press Page Down three times** to move to the text box on page 3.

g.   When the mouse is above the text box on page 3, the mouse pointer resembles a pouring pitcher. 🏺 **Click the text box** to link it to the first text box.

h.   If necessary, **adjust the size of the text box** to accommodate the entire block of text.

4.   Preview the document.

a.   **Click the Office button and choose Print→Print Preview.**

b.   **Scroll through the document** to view the article flowing between the text boxes on different pages.

c.   In the Preview group, **click Close Print Preview.**

d.   **Save the document as** *My Newsletter Box.docx* **and close it.**

Lesson 7 Follow-up

In this lesson, you used different techniques to control the overall flow of text in a document. With these techniques, you can control the overall appearance of any portion of your document to make sure text appears in the right location and in the desired format.

1. **In your own experience, have you seen any examples of text flow control such as text columns, widow/orphan control, and so on?**

2. **Which of the text flow control options do you think you will be using the most in your documents?**

8 Using Templates to Automate Document Creation

Lesson Time: 30 minutes

Lesson Objectives:

In this lesson, you will use templates to automate document creation.

You will:

* Create a document based on a template.
* Create a template.

Introduction

Throughout this course, you have been creating and assembling documents using a number of different document components, such as tables, fields, headers and footers, and boilerplate text. If you create many document that require you to use the same basic components and layouts, you can increase your efficiency and simplify the document creation process by creating the documents from templates. In this lesson, you will use templates to help automate the creation of Word documents.

A standard business document is like a puzzle; you put together pieces such as styles, standard text, specific layout, and graphic options to complete the final effect. If you create the same kind of business documents frequently, you don't need to put those pieces together by hand every time. You can use Word features to put together the key pieces of the document's structure and format automatically.

TOPIC A
Create a Document Based on a Template

In this lesson, you will use templates to automate document creation. Instead of running through all the steps in a wizard to create a document, you may want to base a new document on a specific template. In this topic, you'll create a document based on a Word template.

When starting a new document, you have to set up the margins, choose the styles, plan the general layout, and work on the main document content. If you use a template to do these generic tasks, it will free up your time so that you can concentrate on the content that's specific to your document. By selecting the right template as a basis for your document, you'll feel as if the document is half done as soon as you start it.

Template Categories

Template categories enable you to create documents based on templates that are stored in different locations.

Category	Description
Blank And Recent	Contains options to create new documents and blog entries. The center pane of the dialog box displays the recently used templates.
Installed Templates	Displays various templates that are installed on the local computer. There are also options to create a new document or template based on the installed templates.
My Templates	Displays the New dialog box. The dialog box displays the default global template and the user defined templates. There are also options to create a new document or template based on existing templates.
New From Existing	Displays the New From Existing Document dialog box. The dialog box has options to create a template based on an existing document.
Microsoft Office Online	Displays a list of template types that are available online. Each of these template types has subcategories. Each subcategory, in turn, has several templates that can be used directly in documents. Some templates are for the Office 2003 version of Word; after you create your document, you can save it in the .docx file format.

The Attached Template

When you base a document on a template, the template is attached to the document. As you edit the document, you can access the styles, macros, and other elements in the attached template.

You can view or change the attached template from the Templates And Add-ins dialog box. To open the dialog box, first open the document, and then, in the Word Options dialog box, on the Add-Ins tab, from the Manage drop-down list, select Templates and click Go. The path and name of the currently attached template will appear in the Document Template text box. Click Attach to change the attached template.

When you change the attached template, the current content of the document does not change, but you can now access the styles, macros, and other elements in the new template when you edit the document in the future.

Forms

Forms are Word templates that include special content controls to simplify data entry in the template. For example, forms might have controls that create check boxes, drop-down lists, or placeholder instruction text that a user can replace with a single click. Many of the templates that Microsoft provides include form functionality. For more information on forms and form controls in templates, see the Microsoft Word online Help system.

Template Storage Locations

Except for templates available from Microsoft Office Online, each template category is installed in a specific location on the local computer or local network.

Template Category	Storage Location
Installed templates	By default, Word places locally installed templates on the drive where Windows is installed, in the path \Program Files\Microsoft Office\ Templates\1033.
Default user templates	This is the same folder where the user's personal copy of the Normal.dotm template is located. Each user on a system has a separate default template location and a separate version of Normal.dotm. By default, it will be on the drive where Windows is installed, in the path \Documents And Settings\(username)\Application Data\Microsoft\ Templates. Any other template stored in this location will also appear when you select My Templates in the New Document window.
Downloaded templates	If you base a document on a template that is stored on the Internet, Word will download a copy of the template to your local computer, on the drive where Windows is installed, in the path \Documents And Settings\(username)\Local Settings\Temp. Here, the template will be located in a folder with a name that begins with TC and ends with .tmp.
Workgroup templates	The local network administrator can place templates in a network location.

Template Wizards

Definition:

A *template wizard* is a tool used in previous versions of Word that uses a multi-page format to guide a user through the process of completing the basic information needed to create a document based on a selected template. Microsoft Office Online has several types of template wizards that you can download and use to create a desired type of document. Because wizards are a legacy feature, a document you create from a wizard will open in Compatibility Mode.

Example:

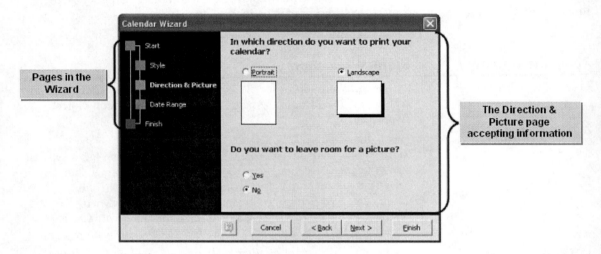

How to Create a Document Based on a Template

Procedure Reference: Create a Document Based on a Template

To create a document based on a template:

1. Click the Office button and choose New.
2. In the New Document dialog box, select the template location.
   - In the left pane, in the Template Categories section, select Installed Templates to select a template from those available on your computer.
   - In the left pane, in the Microsoft Office Online section, select a template category from which you need to select a template from the Microsoft Office Online website.
   - At the top left corner of the dialog box, in the Search text box, enter a search term to search for templates on the Microsoft Office Online website.
3. Open the template.
   - For a local template, click the template, verify that Document is selected under Create New, and click Create.
   - For an online template, select the template and click Download. Click Continue so that Microsoft can validate your copy of Microsoft Office.
4. Edit the default text in the template, as needed, and save the file with the .docx extension.

ACTIVITY 8-1

Creating a Document Based on a Template

Scenario:

You're Heather LaPierre, a property manager at Burke Properties. Jan Burke, the President of Burke Properties, is on vacation and you are handling some of her duties in her absence. Today, you met with Bob Wannamaker from the Creative Associates advertising agency. During the meeting, you and Bob made handwritten changes to some new advertisement copies. You want to fax the changes to Jan for her approval and include a professional-looking cover sheet. You plan to use an origin template format.

What You Do	How You Do It
1. Open a new document based on the Origin Fax template.	a. **Click the Office button and choose New.**
	b. In the New Document dialog box, in the left pane, in the Templates section, **select Installed Templates.**
	c. In the center pane, **scroll down and select the Origin Fax template.**
	d. **Verify that Document is selected and click Create** to open a new document based on the template.

2.	**Edit the text in the template.**	a.	**Double-click the text, Student to select it.**
		b.	If any text appears in the From field, **double-click the text to select it.** (The text is generated by the user name that is set in the Word Options dialog box).
		c.	**Type *Heather LaPierre***

From:¤   ⁞ Heather LaPierre

		d.	**Click [Type The Sender Phone Number] and type *(808) 555–2222***
		e.	**Click [Type The Sender Fax Number] and type *(808) 555–3333***
		f.	You can skip the sender company name. **Click [Type The Recipient Name] and type *Jan Burke***
		g.	**Click [Type The Recipient Phone Number] and type *(808) 555–4444***
		h.	**Click [Type The Recipient Fax Number] and type *(808) 555–1111***
		i.	You can skip the recipient company name. **Click [Type Comments] and type *Let us know what you think.***

3.	**Edit the date.**	a.	**Click [Pick A Date].**
		b.	**Click the drop-down arrow and select today's date.**

4.	**Remove the fields that are not required.**	a.	**Select the sender's Company Name line.**
		b.	**Press Delete** to delete the selected field.
		c.	**Delete the recipient's Company Name line.**
		d.	**Save the document in the Automating Document Creation folder as *My Fax.docx* and close it.**

TOPIC B
Create a Template

You have created documents based on existing templates. You may find that existing templates do not suit your requirements. You can create customized templates to meet your own particular needs. In this topic, you will create templates.

Creating your own custom template gives you an easy and consistent way to incorporate custom elements into new documents. Custom elements might include your own electronic letterhead, sections of standardized text, or a consistent set of formats. By creating a template, you will be able to get the precise results you need for your documents if the built-in Word templates don't exactly meet your needs.

Template Creation Options

You can create a template from an existing document or from another template. Saving a document in the Word Template file format creates a new template based on the existing document. In the New Document dialog box, you can also select a template from the Installed Templates category and make slight modifications to it to create a new template.

The MacroButton Field

If you want to include one-click text-replacement functionality in your template without inserting specific form controls, you can get a similar effect by using the MacroButton field. The MacroButton field is a Word field that is often used in templates to provide automatic prompts and advanced functionality for the template user. Although it can be used to attach a macro (a set of automated tasks) to a document, you can also use it with the *NoMacro* field argument to enable one-click replacement of template text.

The syntax of the MacroButton field is MacroButton *MacroName DisplayText*, where *MacroName* is the macro to run and *DisplayText* is the text that will appear in the document where you insert the field. A user can run the attached macro by double-clicking the display text.

For one-click selection and replacement of boilerplate text in a template, use the *NoMacro* argument instead of a macro name. Your boilerplate text is the DisplayText. For example, you could insert the field MacroButton *NoMacro* "Click here and enter your name" in a letter template to prompt users to type their name at the end of the document.

See the Microsoft Word Help system for more information about the MacroButton field.

The Default Template Location

When you install Microsoft Office Word, the program sets default folder locations for all types of files, including templates. When you begin to create your own templates, you might want to keep them separate from the built-in Word templates, so you might want to change the default template location to point to the folder where you store your custom templates. You can use the File Locations dialog box to change the default template location. On the Advanced tab of the Word Options dialog box, click File Locations, click the file type you want to change the location for, and click Modify.

How to Create a Template

Procedure Reference: Create a Template Based on a Document

To create a template based on a document:

1. Open the Word file on which you want to base the template.
2. If necessary, make changes to the document.
3. Click the Microsoft Office button and choose Save As.
4. In the Save As dialog box, from the Save As Type drop-down list, select Word Template (*.dotx).
5. Select a location for the template. Word automatically changes the Save In location to the default Word templates location.
6. In the File Name text box, specify the file name.
7. Click Save.
8. As a best practice, test the template by opening a new document based on the template.

Procedure Reference: Create a Template Based on an Existing Template

To create a template based on an existing template:

1. Click the Microsoft Office button and choose New.
2. In the New Document dialog box, in the left pane, in the Template Categories section, select Installed Templates.
3. In the center pane, select the template on which you want to base the new template.
4. In the right pane, select the Create New Template option.
5. Click Create to create the template.
6. Make the necessary changes to the newly created template.
7. Save the template in the desired location with a new file name.
8. As a best practice, test the template by opening a new document based on the template.

Procedure Reference: Modify a Template

To modify a template:

1. Use the Open command to open the template in Word.
2. Edit the template as needed.
3. Save the template.

Default Settings in the Normal Template

All of Word's default document settings are stored in the Normal template. This ensures that each new document you create has a consistent look. You can change the default Normal settings by using the Default button in various configuration dialog boxes. For example, you can open a new document, use the Font dialog box to change the font, and click the Default button at the bottom of the dialog box to make your choice the new default font in your personal copy of Normal template.

It is easy to revert to the original Normal template. Close Word, and then delete the version Normal.dotm that is stored in the path \Documents And Settings\(*username*)\Application Data\ Microsoft\Templates, where *username* is the name of your account on the Windows computer. When you re-open Word, the program will create a new copy of Normal.dotm using default settings from the master template.

ACTIVITY 8-2

Creating a Template

Data Files:

Burke Fax.docx

Before You Begin:

From C:\084894Data\Automating Document Creation, open Burke Fax.docx

Scenario:

As a property manager for Burke Properties, you often send cover sheets to accompany contracts and other documents you transmit to clients by fax. You have been using a standard Word fax template to create the cover sheets, but you wish you could quickly create other similar cover sheets that have some of the same standard information you've been entering each time by hand. You decide to remove document-specific information, such as the name, fax number, the number of pages, and comments, from the document so you can use it as the basis for a template.

What You Do	How You Do It
1. **Delete the unnecessary information from the document.**	a. In the document, next to "To:", **select Jan Burke and press Delete.**
	b. Next to "Fax:", **delete Jan Burke's fax number.**
	c. Next to "Pages:", **delete the number of pages.**
	d. Scroll down and, next to "Comments:", **delete the text.** (Leave the Comments heading.)
2. **Save the edited document as a template.**	a. **Click the Office button and choose Save As.**
	b. **Select the Trusted Templates tab.**
	c. In the Save As dialog box, in the File Name text box, **type My Template**
	d. From the Save As Type drop-down list, **select Word Template (*.dotx) and click Save.**
	e. **Close My Template.dotx.**

3. Test the template.

a. **Click the Office button and choose New.**

b. In the left pane, in the Templates section, **select My Templates.**

c. In the New dialog box, on the My Templates tab, **verify that My Template.dotx is selected and click OK.**

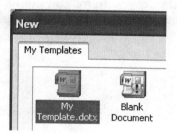

d. **Close the new document without saving the changes.**

Lesson 8 Follow-up

In this lesson, you automated and streamlined the process of document creation using templates. Using a pre-built or custom template can help you create professional-looking documents consistently and efficiently.

1. **Do you think you will find templates useful for the documents with which you work?**

2. **Which elements do you think you might need to include in a custom template for the documents you work with on a daily basis?**

9 | Automating Mail Merges

Lesson Time: 45 minutes

Lesson Objectives:

In this lesson, you will perform mail merges.

You will:

- Perform a mail merge.
- Merge envelopes and labels.
- Create a data source.

Introduction

In the previous lesson, you created templates so that you can easily create similar documents quickly. In some cases, you will need to create many documents that are generally similar, but are customized for individual recipients. In this lesson, you will perform mail merges to produce a variety of customized documents.

Mail merge is a great tool if you need to produce a lot of similar documents that need just a little bit of customization. Maybe you personalize cover letters to include with each customer's billing statement. Maybe you run labels for bulk mailings. Instead of creating each one of these documents individually, you can use a mail merge to produce them all in a few simple steps.

TOPIC A
Perform a Mail Merge

In this lesson, you will automate document creation by using mail merges. In the simplest case, you will have documents ready to merge and all you will need to do is perform the merge and generate the output. In this topic, you will perform a mail merge on existing documents.

Creating hundreds of similar letters where the only content that varies is the name and address can be a time consuming task, especially when you have a long list of recipients. By performing a mail merge, you can produce stacks of eye-catching customized documents in a fraction of the time it would take you to create each one by hand.

Mail Merge

Definition:

Mail merge is a word processor feature that produces multiple individualized documents from a master document and a separate source of data. The master document is called the *main merge document;* it contains both fixed data and placeholder fields to display variable data. The merge produces multiple customized documents, each combining the static data with content from the data source that replaces the placeholder fields. You can use mail merge in Word to create a wide variety of customized documents including letters, emails, envelopes, labels, or even a company phone book.

Sweepstakes letters from a magazine publisher, with customized names and addresses for each recipient, are created using a mail merge.

Example:

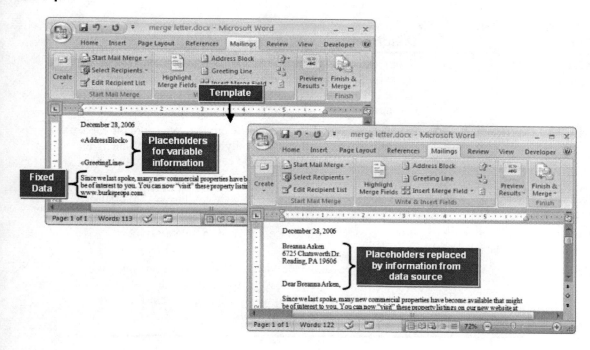

Merge Fields

Definition:

A *merge field* is a placeholder for variable content in a main merge document. These placeholders link the document to a data source, which contains the variable information to be merged. A merge field is indicated by double arrows before and after the field name. There can be multiple merge fields in a main merge document.

Example:

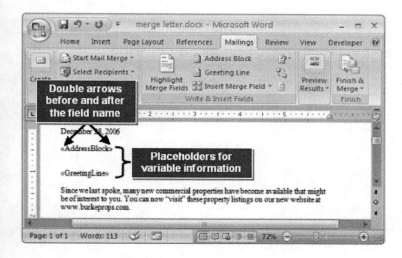

Types of Merge Fields

You can insert any of the following merge fields into your main document:

Field Name (Field Code)	Description
Address Block (AddressBlock)	Inserts name and address information from the data source to create an address. Word will either automatically determine which fields in the data source contain the name and address or will prompt you to match the fields manually.
Greeting Line (GreetingLine)	Inserts the name of the recipient from the data source to create a greeting. Word will automatically determine which fields in the data source contain the name or prompt you to match the fields manually.
Electronic Postage (no field code)	Adds postage to mailings if an electronic postage program is installed.
More Items (varies according to field name in data source)	Inserts content from a specified field in a data source.
Rules	Introduces programmatic logic to add decision-making ability into the mail merge process. One example is the "Skip Record If (SkipIf)" field. Refer to the Word Help system for more information on advanced Word fields.

Data Sources

Definition:

A *data source* is a collection of information that forms the input for the merge. The data source must contain a row of field names followed by rows of information that contain the information for the fields. The data source can be a variety of database types including Outlook Contacts lists, Excel worksheets, Word tables, or Access database tables.

Example:

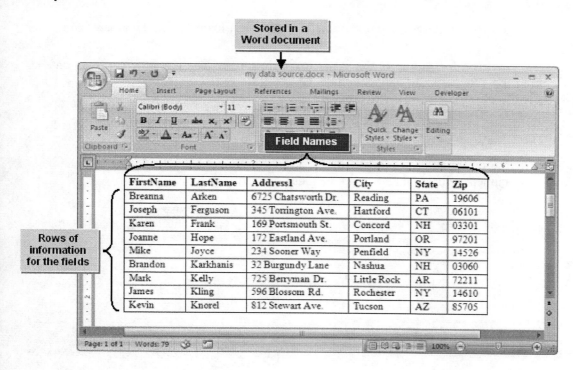

Data Source File Types

You can type the data source as you run the merge, but if you create the data source before the merge and store it in a file, you can ensure that it is structured correctly. Word supports the following file types as data sources:

● A Microsoft Outlook Contacts list.

● Address books from other email clients.

● An Office Address List (a list that you type during the merge process).

● A table in an Excel worksheet. The worksheet can contain multiple data source tables, each on a separate sheet.

● A table in an Access database.

● Tables in other databases, such as Microsoft Office Query or Microsoft Office FoxPro.

● A table in an HTML file (a Web page file).

● A table in a Word document. The table must contain a header row with the field names, and data rows containing the merge data.

● A *delimited text file* . This is a plain text file in which the fields in each row are separated by a comma or tab character, and each row of data is separated by a carriage return. The first line in the file must contain the field names.

The Mail Merge Process

The mail merge process merges data from a data source to a main merge document using four general steps.

1. Entering text and formatting in the main merge document. The text could be the content required for a letter, email, envelope or a label.

2. Creating the data source. The data source can be an existing one or created by the user.

3. Inserting fields in the main document to link it to the data source. The fields inserted should correspond to the information in the data source.

4. Merging the information to produce the customized output. The data source and the main merge document will be linked to produce customized results.

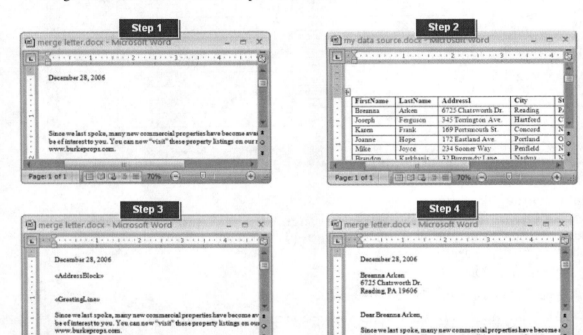

Figure 9-1: *The general steps in the mail merge process.*

The Mailings Tab

The mail merge process can be performed using the various options in the groups on the Mailings tab. You can select the recipients list to use as a data source; insert merge fields into a merge document; create envelope and label main documents; and start, preview, and complete the merge.

The Mail Merge Wizard

You can also use the Step By Step Mail Merge Wizard option in the Start Mail Merge group of the Mailings tab to complete the merge process in a series of six steps.

Wizard Step	Enables You To
Step 1 Of 6	Select a document type, such as letters, envelopes, or labels for a group mailing. You can also select a directory to print a list of addresses in a single document.
Step 2 Of 6	Select a starting document. You can select the current document, an existing document, or a template on which the mail merge will be performed.
Step 3 Of 6	Select the details from an existing list, an Outlook contacts list, or create a new list for the data source information of the mail merge.
Step 4 Of 6	Insert merge fields, such as Address block, Greeting Line, Electronic Postage, and other database fields.
Step 5 Of 6	Preview the mail-merged document. You can view each document type separately with its unique contact details. It is also possible to exclude or edit contacts at this point.
Step 6 Of 6	Print, save, or edit the resultant document of your merge.

Saving the Main Document and Resuming a Merge

At any time during your merge, you can save the original main merge document. This will save the inserted merge field codes and a link to the data source along with the document contents. You might do this if you want to resume the merge process at a later time. When you open the main merge document after saving it, Word will also open the associated data source. You can then open the Mail Merge task pane and complete the merge.

If Word cannot locate the data source, it will prompt you to open the data source manually. If you do not want to open the data source or resume the merge, in the Microsoft Office Word dialog box, click Options.

- Click Remove Data/Header Source to break the link between the two documents, but leave the merge codes. Do this if you want to merge a different data source into this main document.

- Click Remove All Merge Info to remove the merge field codes and convert the document back to an ordinary Word document. Do this if you no longer need to use this document as the basis for a merge.

Creating a Main Document

The only way in which a main document differs from an ordinary Word document is that the main document contains merge fields. Because you can insert merge fields during the merge process, there are no special steps you need to take before the merge to create a main merge document. However, if you prefer, you can insert the fields into the document manually, prior to the merge, using the Mailings tab on the Ribbon. If you create the main merge document ahead of time, you can ensure that it is structured correctly.

Merge Dialog Boxes

There are several dialog boxes you might use during the merge process.

Dialog Box	Description
Insert Merge Fields	The Insert Merge Fields dialog box allows you to add additional fields into your main document from your data source. This dialog box can be displayed by either clicking Insert Merge Fields in the Write & Insert Fields group or by selecting More Items in Step 4 Of 6 in the Mail Merge Wizard. You can select either of the two insert options, Address Fields or Database Fields. The Address Fields option is used to select from a list of built-in merge fields that may not have the same name as the fields in your data source. You can also use the Database Fields options to select from a list of merge fields that link to fields of the same name present in your data file.
Mail Merge Recipients	The Mail Merge Recipients dialog box enables you to edit the recipients list once you have specified a data source. This dialog box displays a list of all the fields and data in the data source. You can perform simple sorting and filtering, or exclude individual recipients.
Filter and Sort	You can use the Filter And Sort dialog box to perform an advanced sort or filter on the data in the data source. On the Filter Records tab, you can select the field to filter by, a comparison operator, and comparison text to filter against. On the Sort Records tab, you can choose multiple fields to sort by, the order in which to sort the fields, and the ascending or descending direction of the sort for each field.

How to Perform a Mail Merge

Procedure Reference: Start a Merge Using the Mail Merge Wizard

To start a merge using the Mail Merge Wizard:

1. Open a blank document or the existing document you wish to use as the main merge document.

2. On the Mailings tab, in the Start Mail Merge group, click Start Mail Merge and choose Step By Step Mail Merge Wizard to start the mail merge wizard.

    *   The Mail Merge wizard will open at Step 1 Of 6 of the wizard, if you have a blank document open, or if Word cannot determine the merge document type.

    *   The Mail Merge wizard will open at Step 3 Of 6 of the wizard, if you have an existing main merge document open and Word can determine the document type.

Procedure Reference: Select the Main Merge Document Type

To select the document type:

1. In Step 1 Of 6 of the Mail Merge wizard pane, in the Select Document Type section, select the type of document you are working on: Letters, E-mail Messages, Envelopes, or Labels, or select Directory to create one document containing the variable information as a list or catalog.

2. At the bottom of the Mail Merge wizard pane, click the Next: Starting Document link to move to Step 2 Of 6.

3. In the Select Starting Document section, select the way in which you want to set up your chosen document type.

    *   If your chosen document type is a letter, email, or directory, you can use the current document, start from a built-in mail merge template, or start from another existing document.

    *   If your chosen document type is an envelope or a label, you can use the current document, start from another existing document, or select Change Document Layout to use a built-in mail merge template and to format the size of the envelope or label.

4. At the bottom of the wizard pane, click the Next: Select Recipients link to move to Step 3 Of 6.

Procedure Reference: Select the Recipients for the Mail Merge

To select the recipients for the mail merge:

1. In Step 3 Of 6 of the Mail Merge wizard pane, in the Select Recipients section, select the data source. You can use an existing list in Word, Excel, or Access; an Outlook email contacts list; or type a new list.

2. To filter or sort the data source, click the Edit Recipient List link to open the Mail Merge Recipients dialog box.

    *   To perform a one-level sort, click the desired column heading. Text fields will be sorted alphabetically from A to Z; number fields will be sorted numerically from lowest to highest.

    *   To perform a simple filter, click the drop-down arrow next to any field name and select the appropriate option.

    *   To perform an advanced sort or filter, click the drop-down arrow next to any field name, click Advanced to open the Filter And Sort dialog box, and make the appropriate selections.

        a. On the Sort Records tab, specify the sort fields and sort order.

        b. On the Filter Records tab, select the field you want to filter by, select the comparison operator, and enter the value to filter by.

            *   Select All to display all the recipients in the data source.

            *   Select Blanks to show only recipients with blank information in that field.

            *   Select Nonblanks to show only recipients with information in that field.

        c. Click OK to close the Filter And Sort dialog box.

    *   Uncheck the check boxes for any individual recipients you want to exclude.

3. If necessary, click OK to close the Mail Merge Recipients dialog box.

4. At the bottom of the wizard pane, click the Next link to move to Step 3 Of 6.

Procedure Reference: Insert Merge Fields into the Document

To insert merge fields into the document:

1. In the document, position your insertion point where you want the field to appear.

2. In Step 4 Of 6 of the Mail Merge Wizard pane, click the link to the field you wish to insert.

- In the Write Your Letter section, click a standard merge field, such as AddressBlock or GreetingLine.
- Click More Items to insert fields directly from your data source. Select the field name, click Insert, and then click Close.

 If the Match Fields dialog box appears, Word might not be able to map the standard merge field to the fields in your data source. Use the dialog box to select the correct fields.

3. For standard merge fields, use the dialog box for the field to make any changes to the default settings for that field.

4. Click OK in the dialog box for the field to insert the field.

5. Repeat as necessary for other merge fields.

6. At the bottom of the wizard pane, click the Next link to move to Step 5 Of 6. The data is merged together.

Procedure Reference: Complete the Merge

To complete the merge:

1. In Step 5 of the Mail Merge Wizard, in the Preview section, click the Next and Previous buttons to preview the output for each recipient.

- In the Make Changes section, click the Exclude This Recipient button to exclude a selected recipient.
- In the Make Changes section, click the Edit Recipient List link to modify the recipient list.

2. At the bottom of the wizard pane, click the Next: Complete The Merge link to move to Step 6 Of 6.

3. If necessary, print the completed document.

a. In the Merge section, click the Print link.

b. In the Merge To Printer dialog box, select the records to print and click OK.

c. In your printer's Print dialog box, click OK.

4. If you want to print the merged document later or edit it directly, save the completed document.

a. Click Edit Individual Letters to make changes to a particular record.

b. Select the records to save and click OK to create a new document containing the selected records.

c. Save the new document.

ACTIVITY 9-1

Performing a Mail Merge

Data Files:

Merge Letter.docx, Mailing List.xlsx

Before You Begin:

You have a print driver installed and configured as your default printer.

Scenario:

You need to create personalized letters for commercial property customers in the New York State territory. You want to arrange the completed letters in a logical order. You address all your customers on a first name basis. As you create the letters, you realize you are already closing a commercial property deal with one customer, Elizabeth Milko.

What You Do	How You Do It
1. Select the Merge Letter document as the main merge document.	a. **Open a blank, new document and display formatting marks.**
	b. In the Microsoft Word window, on the Mailings tab, in the Start Mail Merge group, **click Start Mail Merge and choose Step By Step Mail Merge Wizard** to open the Mail Merge wizard pane.
	c. In the Mail Merge wizard pane, in the Select Document Type section, **verify that the Letters option is selected and at the bottom of the pane, click the Next: Starting Document link.**
	d. In the Select Starting Document section, **select the Start From Existing Document option** to open an existing main merge document.
	e. In the Start From Existing section, **click Open.**
	f. In the Open dialog box, **navigate to C:\084894Data\Automating Mail Merges** and **open Merge Letter.docx.**

2. Select Sheet 1 of the Mailing List workbook as the data source.

a. In the Mail Merge Wizard pane, at the bottom of the pane, **click the Next: Select Recipients link** to move to Step 3 Of 6 of the wizard.

b. In the Select Recipients section, **verify that the Use An Existing List option is selected** and in the Use An Existing List section, **click the Browse link.**

c. The default location for data sources is the My Data Sources subfolder. **Navigate to C:\084894Data\Automating Mail Merges and open Mailing List.xlsx.**

d. In the Select Table dialog box, **click OK** to open Sheet1$ of the Excel workbook and display the data.

LastName	FirstName	Address1	City
Myszka	A.J.	65286 Milestrip Rd.	Fairfield
Smolkovich	Anne	693 Northcutt Blvd.	Burlington
Willenbecher	Ben	87 Country Lane	Charlottesville
Karkhanis	Brandon	32 Burgundy Lane	Nashua
Arken	Breanna	6725 Chatsworth Dr.	Reading
Santos	Carlos	145 Windsor Dr.	Alexandria
Olsen	Carol	209 Parrish St.	Eugene
Neyman	Darcy	159 Rutgers St.	Dayton
Milko	Elizabeth	23 Pebble Beach Rd.	Lakeville
Kling	James	595 Blossom Rd.	Rochester
Hope	Joanne	172 Eastland Ave.	Portland

3. Modify the data source to include only customers from New York alphabetically sorted by last name.

a. In the Mail Merge Recipients dialog box, **click the LastName column heading** to sort the list alphabetically by last name.

 Click the words in the heading, not the drop-down arrow.

b. **Scroll to the right and click the drop-down arrow next to the State column heading.**

c. From the menu, **choose (Advanced)** to display the Filter And Sort dialog box.

d. On the Filter Records tab, from the Field drop-down list, **select State.**

e. In the Comparison drop-down list, **verify that the default comparison operator is set to Equal To.**

f. In the Compare To text box, **type *NY***

g. **Click OK** to filter the recipients list so that only the New York customers are included.

h. In the Mail Merge Recipients dialog box, **scroll to the right** to verify that the filtered list shows five clients with addresses in New York State. **Click OK.**

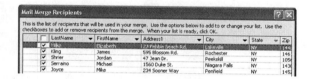

4. **Insert the address block with the first and last name of the recipient.**

| If field codes appear in the main merge document instead of field results, press Alt+F9.

a. In the Mail Merge Wizard pane, **click the Next: Write Your Letter link.**

b. In the Microsoft Word document, **position the insertion point before the second empty paragraph mark after the date.**

c. In the Mail Merge wizard pane, in the Write Your Letter section, **click the Address Block link** to open the Insert Address Block dialog box.

d. In the Specify Address Elements section, in the Insert Recipient's Name In This Format list box, **verify that the fifth sample format in the list is selected.**

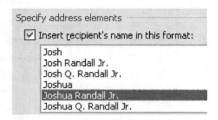

e. **Click OK** to insert the AddressBlock field in the letter.

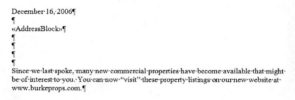

---

5. Insert the greeting field.

a. In the Microsoft Word document, **position the insertion point before the third empty paragraph mark after the AddressBlock field.**

 There will be an empty paragraph mark after the greeting line and before the body of the letter.

b. In the Mail Merge wizard pane, in the Write Your Letter section, **click the Greeting Line link.**

c. In the Insert Greeting Line dialog box, in the Greeting Line Format section, from the second drop-down list, **scroll down and select the greeting line format that reads simply "Joshua".**

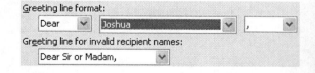

d. **Click OK** to insert the Greeting Line field into the document.

December·16,·2006¶

¶

«AddressBlock»¶

¶

¶

¶

¶

Since·we·last·spoke,·

to·you.·You·can·now·

---

6. **Exclude Elizabeth Milko as a recipient.**

a. In the Mail Merge wizard pane, at the bottom of the pane, **click the Next: Preview Your Letters link.**

b. In the Preview Your Letters section, **click the Next Recipient button** `>>` **four times** to preview all the letters in the Document1 - Microsoft Word window.

c. In the Mail Merge wizard pane, in the Preview Your Letters section, **click the Previous Recipient button twice** to return to the letter for Recipient 3, Elizabeth Milko.

d. In the Make Changes section, **click Exclude This Recipient.**

---

7. **Print the completed letters.**

a. At the bottom of the Mail Merge wizard pane, **click the Next: Complete The Merge link.**

b. In the Merge section, **click the Print link** to open the Merge To Printer dialog box.

c. In the Print Records section, **verify that the All option is selected and click OK** to open the Print dialog box.

d. **Click OK** to send the letters to the default printer.

---

8. **Convert the main merge document into individual letters.**

    a. In the Mail Merge wizard pane, in the Merge section, **click the Edit Individual Letters link** to open the Merge To New Document dialog box.

    b. In the Merge Records section, **verify that the All option is selected and click OK.**

    c. In the Letters1 - Microsoft Word window, **scroll down** to observe that the new document contains each letter on its own page.

    d. **Save the new document as *My Mail Merge.docx* and close it.**

    e. In the Mail Merge wizard pane, **click the Close button** to exit the wizard.

    f. **Close the Word document without saving the changes.**

TOPIC B
Mail Merge Envelopes and Labels

You have worked with merging data to create a customized letter. You might also want to create customized envelopes and labels. In this topic, you will merge envelopes and labels.

You've probably already realized that performing a mail merge is the fastest and easiest way to create any quantity of mailing labels or envelopes. With a simple main merge document and a data source for the addresses, it's easy to use the merge function to create and print envelopes and labels for many recipients.

Merge Options for Envelopes and Labels

You can set the merge and printing options for envelopes in the Envelope Options dialog box. You can choose the envelope size, set the font and positioning for delivery and return addresses, and preview your envelopes.

You can set the merge options for labels in the Label Options dialog box. You can set printing options, select or view details about a built-in label format, or create a custom label.

How to Merge Envelopes and Labels
Procedure Reference: Merge Envelopes or Labels

To merge envelopes or labels:

1. Open a blank document.
2. On the Mailings tab, in the Start Mail Merge group, click Start Mail Merge and select Step By Step Mail Merge Wizard.
3. In the Mail Merge Wizard pane, in the Select Document Type section, select the Envelopes or Labels option.
4. At the bottom of the Mail Merge Wizard pane, click the Next: Starting Document link.
5. In the Change Document Layout section, click the Envelope Options or the Label Options link to display the Envelope Options or Label Options dialog box.
6. For envelopes, specify the envelope size and address appearance.
   - From the Envelope Size drop-down list, select the desired envelope size. The default envelope size is 10 (4⅛″ by 9½″).
   - In the Delivery Address and Return Address sections, select a font for each address and specify how the address should be positioned in relation to the left and top margins.
7. For labels, select the label type.
   - From the Label Vendors drop-down list, select a label vendor.
   - From the Product Number drop-down list, select the desired product number from that label vendor.
8. Click OK to close the Envelope Options or Label Options dialog box.
9. In the wizard pane, at the bottom of the pane, click the Next: Select Recipients link.
10. Select the recipients from the data source as you would in any mail merge.

11. At the bottom of the pane, click the Next: Arrange Your Envelope link or the Next: Arrange Your Labels link.

12. In the document, place the insertion point in the envelope or one of the labels and insert the desired merge fields into it.

13. For labels, in the wizard pane, in the Replicate Labels section, click Update All Labels to copy the merge fields to the other labels.

14. Preview, save, or print your merged envelopes or labels as you would in any mail merge.

Procedure Reference: Print a Single Envelope Using the Ribbon

To print an envelope using the ribbon:

1. On the Mailings tab, in the Create group, click Envelopes to open the Envelopes And Labels dialog box.

2. On the Envelopes tab, in the Delivery Address text box, type in the required address.

3. Click Print.

Procedure Reference: Print a Single Label

To print a single label:

1. On the Mailings tab, in the Create group, click Labels to display the Envelopes And Labels dialog box.

2. In the Envelopes And Labels dialog box, select the Labels tab.

3. In the Print section, select the Single Label option, and click Print.

ACTIVITY 9-2
Merging Labels

Data Files:

Mailing List.xlsx

Before You Begin:

You have a print driver installed and configured as your default printer.

Scenario:

Burke Properties uses labels to address company mailings. Your company used the Avery Standard label in the past. The labels will have the first and last name of the recipient with no titles. Also, you have been asked to exclude Elizabeth Milko from the recipients list.

What You Do	How You Do It
1. Create a new label document as the main document.	a. **Open a new blank document.**
	b. On the Mailings tab, in the Start Mail Merge group, **click Start Mail Merge and choose Step By Step Mail Merge Wizard.**
	c. In the Mail Merge wizard pane, in the Select Document Type section, **select the Labels option.**
	d. At the bottom of the wizard pane, **click the Next: Starting Document link.**
	e. In the Select Starting Document section, **verify that the Change Document Layout option is selected** and in the Change Document Layout section, **click the Label Options link.**
	f. In the Label Options dialog box, in the Label Information section, from the Label Vendors drop-down list, **select Avery A4/A5.**

g. In the Product Number list, **scroll down and select EM8160. Click OK.**

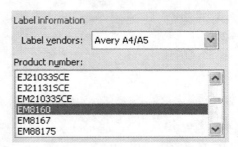

---

2. **Select the data source.**

    a. At the bottom of the wizard pane, **click the Next: Select Recipients link.**

    b. In the Select Recipients section, **verify that the Use An Existing List option is selected** and in the Use An Existing List section, **click the Browse link.**

    c. In the Select Data Source dialog box, **navigate to C:\084894Data\Automating Mail Merges and open Mailing List.xlsx.**

    d. In the Select Table dialog box, **click OK** to open Sheet1$ of the Excel workbook as the data source.

---

3. **Configure the recipients list so that the label output matches the merged letters.**

    a. In the Mail Merge Recipients dialog box, **click the LastName column heading** to sort the list alphabetically by last name.

 Click the words in the heading, not the drop-down arrow.

b. **Scroll to the right and click the drop-down arrow next to the State column heading.**

c. **Select (Advanced).**

d. In the Filter and Sort dialog box, on the Filter Records tab, **click the Field drop-down arrow and select State.**

e. In the Compare To text box, **type *NY* and click OK.**

f. **Uncheck the check box for Elizabeth Milko** to exclude her from the merge.

g. In the Mail Merge Recipients dialog box, **click OK.**

---

4. **Insert the address block.**

a. **Click Next: Arrange Your Labels** to move to the Step 4 Of 6 Mail Merge task pane.

b. **Verify that the insertion point is on the empty paragraph mark in the first label on the page.**

c. In the Arrange Your Labels section, **click Address Block** to open the Insert Address Block dialog box.

d. From the Insert Recipient's Name In This Format list, **verify that the choice for first and last name with no title is selected and click OK** to insert the address block field in the first label.

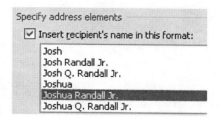

e. In the Mail Merge task pane, in the Replicate Labels section, **click Update All Labels** to copy the AddressBlock field to the other labels on the page.

---

5. **Preview and print the labels.**

a. **Click Next: Preview Your Labels** to move to the Step 5 Of 6 Mail Merge task pane.

b. At the bottom of the wizard pane, **click the Next: Complete The Merge link.**

c. In the Merge section, **click the Print link.**

d. In the Merge To Printer dialog box, in the Print Records section, **verify that the All option is selected and click OK** to open the Print dialog box.

e. **Click OK** to send the labels to the default printer.

f. In the Mail Merge wizard pane, **click the Close button** to exit the wizard.

g. **Close the document without saving the changes.**

OPTIONAL DISCOVERY ACTIVITY 9-3
Merging Envelopes

Activity Time: 5 minutes

Data Files:

Mailing List.xlsx

Before You Begin:

You have a print driver installed and configured as your default printer.

Scenario:

After creating the form letters, you have to print the addresses directly on envelopes. The envelopes will have the first and last name of the recipient with no titles. Since you have excluded Elizabeth Milko as a recipient in your form letters, the same has to be done for the envelopes.

---

1. **Create a new envelope document as the main document.**

---

2. **Select Mailing List as the data source.**

---

3. **Configure the recipients list so that the envelope output matches the merged letters.**

---

4. **Insert the address block.**

---

5. **Preview and print the envelopes.**

TOPIC C
Use Word to Create a Data Source

You have completed a merge using an existing data source. You can also create your own data sources using a number of different applications. In this topic, you will use create a data source using Word.

In many cases, your merge data source will already be provided. Maybe you're using your Outlook contacts list or your company's Microsoft® Office Access™ database. What if none of those data sources already exist? In cases like these, you can use Word to create a personalized data source for yourself. If you know how to structure a data source document in Word, you'll always have the information you need to complete your merges successfully, and you can use the same principles to set up data sources properly in other applications as well.

How to Create a Data Source

Procedure Reference: Create a Data Source Using Word

To create a data source using Word:

1. Open a new blank document.
2. In the document, insert a table with the number of columns that equals the number of fields you need for your data source.
3. Using the data source field name guidelines, type column headings in each column of the table to create field names.
4. Type the data in separate rows in the table.
5. Save the document.
6. If necessary, test the data source by performing a merge.

Data Source Field Naming Guidelines

Use the following guidelines when you create the field names in your data source:

● Make each field name unique within the data source.
● Begin all field names with a letter.
● Make field names as short as possible. Field names cannot exceed 40 characters.
● Do not use spaces in field names.

ACTIVITY 9-4
Creating a Data Source

Scenario:

Jan Burke wants to let three outstanding Burke Properties sales representatives know that their personal share of their home sales commission is going to increase. Jan has asked you to tabulate all the details about the representatives; she will personalize these details as memos and send them herself.

Your data source will look like the following graphic.

FName	LName	Current	New
Jennifer	Allen	3%	4%
James	Hickey	3.5%	4%
Michelle	Robinson	3%	3.5%

What You Do	How You Do It
1. Create the data source document.	a. **Open a new blank document.** b. **Insert a table with four columns and four rows.** c. In the table, in the first column, in the first cell, **type *FName* and press Tab.** d. In the second column, in the first cell, **type *LName* and press Tab.** e. In the third column, in the first cell, **type *Current* and press Tab.** f. In the fourth column, in the first cell, **type *New* and press Tab.**

2. **Type the data for the sales representatives.**

    a. Using the graphic in the scenario as a guide, **type the data for Jennifer Allen, whose sales commission percentage is increasing from 3% to 4%.**

    b. **Type the data for James Hickey, whose percentage is increasing from 3.5% to 4%.**

    c. **Type the data for Michelle Robinson, whose percentage is increasing from 3% to 3.5%.**

    d. **Save the document in the Automating Mail Merges folder as *My Data Source.docx*** in the lesson folder **and close it.**

DISCOVERY ACTIVITY 9-5
Testing the Data Source

Data Files:

Commission Memo.docx

Before You Begin:

From C:\084894Data\Automating Mail Merges open Commission Memo.docx.

Scenario:

You've created the memo and the data source for Jan Burke. She wants to personalize the final product. You want to be sure that the documents can merge successfully so that Jan can simply resume the merge at a later time to personalize the memos as she wishes.

1. Select Commission Memo as the main document.

2. Specify the document you created as the data source.

3. Insert a greeting line on the To line.

4. Insert a field for the current commission rate.

5. Insert a field for the new commission rate.

6. Preview the documents and save the merge.

Lesson 9 Follow-up

In this lesson, you performed mail merges. Once you know how to perform all the steps of a merge successfully, you will probably find many applications for the mail merge technique. Think of using a merge any time you have documents that share most of the same text. Chances are, you'll be able to set up a merge and produce all the customized documents you need in a fraction of the time it would take to type each one individually.

1. **How will you use mail merge?**

2. **What ideas do you have for using mail merge in projects other than mailings?**

10 Using Macros to Automate Tasks

Lesson Time: 30 minutes

Lesson Objectives:

In this lesson, you will use macros to automate common tasks.

You will:

* Perform a task automatically using a macro.
* Create a macro.

Introduction

You have used a number of tools in this course to automate your work so that you can become a more efficient user of Word. The ultimate in automation is to reduce your common, repetitive tasks to a single command called a macro that you can invoke with a click of a mouse or the press of a key. In this lesson, you will automate common Word tasks by using macros.

As a proficient Word user, you may begin to find that there are tasks specific to your work flow that you perform over and over again. Perhaps you apply the same custom paragraph style frequently, create the same customized headers or footers, or often set the same text wrapping properties on a picture you've inserted. It would be nice to perform those specialized tasks at the touch of a button. By automating the tasks you perform every day, you can get more work done in less time.

TOPIC A

Perform a Task Automatically Using a Macro

You are familiar with performing various tasks using the Word application. You would like to automate the process of performing some of the tasks that are redundant on the job. In this topic, you will run macros to perform tasks automatically.

There may be tasks that you do over and over again that are specific to your work environment. For instance, if all your company mail should include the current date, company address, logo, and some standard text at the end of the letter, then you might want to automate this task using simple commands instead of typing or inserting them manually. Many companies create and distribute macros so that employees can perform these tasks quickly and consistently. If you have job-specific automation tools available in your work environment, knowing how to run them successfully can be a great time-saving tool.

Macros

Definition:

A *macro* is a task automation tool that executes a set of commands to automate frequently repeated steps. Each macro is uniquely identified by a macro name. You can use the macro recorder to record a sequence of actions and then perform these tasks by initiating a simple command assigned to the macro. Macros can be stored in documents or in templates. If a macro needs to be made available across all Word documents, it has to be stored in the global template. A macro-enabled Word document has a file name extension of .docm, instead of .docx. Macro controls are available in the Code group on the Developer tab of the Ribbon.

Example:

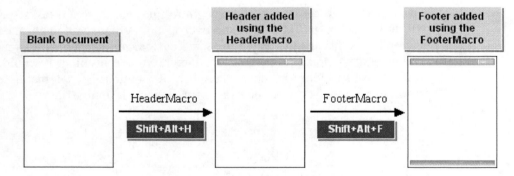

The Macros Dialog Box

The Macros dialog box provides options to work with existing macros or create new ones. It displays the name and description of the currently selected macro, names of other macros in the document or template, and a list of other locations to find macros. It provides controls to run, create, or delete macros; step through macro code; edit macro code directly; and organize how macros are stored within documents and templates.

Macro Security

Because macros contain programming code, they have the potential to produce harmful effects on your system. These effects can be caused inadvertently by improper macro construction. They can also be caused deliberately if the macro writer uses the macro code as a delivery method for malicious programs, such as computer viruses. To reduce the risk of unsafe macros, Microsoft has constructed a macro security system that enables you to disable macros that are potentially unsafe. A disabled macro cannot run, which means that unsafe code in the macro cannot execute, thus protecting your system. Macros are enabled or disabled when you open the document or load the template that contains the macros. You can manage macro security settings in the Trust Center dialog box.

Macro Security System Components

The macro security system incorporates various elements.

Component	Description
Trusted locations	These are local or network folders that contain macros that will run without being evaluated by the Trust Center. There are default trusted locations in Word, and you can create other trusted locations.
Trusted publishers	These are individuals or organizations whose macros you deem safe. You can view or remove trusted publishers in the Trust Center.
Digital signature	This is a small amount of electronic code included with a macro to identify the publisher of the macro. You cannot trust the publisher of a macro that is not digitally signed, but if you choose to trust a publisher of a macro that is signed, the publisher will be added to your Trusted Publishers list.
Macro security levels	This is the Word setting that determines how Word will handle macros that are not trusted. You can disable them all; disable them but receive notification when a macro tries to run; disable macros without digital signatures; or enable all macros. The default setting is to disable macros with notification.

How to Perform a Task Automatically Using a Macro

Procedure Reference: Run a Macro

To run a macro:

1. Open the document in the location you are going to run the macro.
2. Click Enable Macros if you are prompted to enable or disable macros in the document.
3. If the Developer tab does not appear on the Ribbon, display it.
   a. Click the Microsoft Office button and click Word Options.
   b. In the Word Options dialog box, select Popular and check the Show Developer Tab In The Ribbon check box.
   c. Click OK.
4. Display the Macros dialog box.
   - On the Developer tab, in the Code group, click Macros.
   - Or, on the View tab, in the Macros group, click the Macros button.
5. Select the name of the macro you want to run. By default, all macros in all active documents and templates are listed.
6. Click Run.

Storing Macros in the Global Template

To run a macro, it must be stored either in the open document or in the global template. To store a macro in the global template so that you can run it in any open document, you can use the Organizer in the Macros dialog box to select and copy specific macros from a selected document or template into the global template. Or, you can click Document Template on the Developer tab to open the Templates And Add-ins dialog box, click Add, and add a macro-enabled document into the global template.

Procedure Reference: Set the Security Level of a Macro from an Untrusted Location

To set the security level of a macro in a document that is not stored in a trusted location:

1. Open the Trust Center.
   - On the Developer tab, in the Code group, click Macro Security.
   - Or, open the Word Options dialog box, select the Trust Center tab, and click Trust Center settings.
2. On the Macro Settings tab, select the desired level of security, and click OK.

ACTIVITY 10-1

Performing a Task Automatically Using a Macro

Data Files:

Burke Name.docx

Scenario:

Burke Properties has recently trademarked the company name. All company literature, both internal and external, needs to be updated with the new trademarked name, Burke Properties™. The technical support team has created and distributed a file, Automating Tasks, which contains a macro that automates this process. You have not used macros before. The team assures you that this macro, although not signed, is safe to run, but that, in general, you should not run untrusted macros.

What You Do	How You Do It
1. Display the Developer tab.	a. **Click the Office button and choose Word Options.**
	b. If necessary, **click the Popular tab.**
	c. **Check the Show Developer Tab In The Ribbon check box and click OK.**
	d. **Select the Developer tab.**
2. Enable all macros to run.	a. On the Developer tab, in the Code group, **click Macro Security.**
	b. In the Trust Center dialog box, on the Macro Settings tab, **select Enable All Macros option and click OK.**
3. Examine the company names in the Burke Name document.	a. From C:\084894Data\Automating Tasks, **open Burke Name.docx.**

b. **Scroll down** to verify that Burke Properties does not include the trademark symbol.

Burke Properties
We'll find the right property for you!

About Burke Properties
Founded in 1946 by John Burke, Burke Properties is a full-service real estate agency. Not only do we buy and sell residential and commercial properties, Burke Properties can also handle your leasing and relocation needs.

---

4. **Store the macro from the Automating Tasks document in the default global template.**

a. On the Developer tab, in the Templates group, **click Document Template.**

b. In the Templates And Add-Ins dialog box, in the Document Template section, **verify that the default global template, Normal, is selected.**

c. In the Global Templates And Add-Ins section, **click Add** to display the Add Template dialog box.

d. **Navigate to C:\084894Data\Automating Tasks, select Automating Tasks.dotm and click OK.**

e. **Verify that the check box next to the file name is checked and click OK** to add the NameChange macro to the default template.

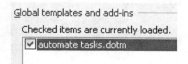

---

5. **Run the NameChange macro in the Burke Name document.**

a. On the Developer tab in the Code group, **click Macros.**

---

b. With the NameChange macro selected, **click Run** to run the macro.

c. **Press Page Down** to verify that the company name now appears as *Burke Properties™*.

d. **Save the document as *My Burke Name.docx*** and close it.

---

6. **Disable untrusted macros.**

a. On the Developer tab, in the Code group, **click Macro Security.**

b. In the Trust Center dialog box, on the Macro Settings tab, **select Disable All Macros With Notification option and click OK.**

TOPIC B

Create a Macro

You executed macros which have already been created. To automate certain tasks that you perform often, you want to create your own personalized macros. In this topic, you will create macros in Word.

What tasks do you perform over and over? Perhaps you search for and replace the same text frequently, add a standard header or footer, or insert the date using a specific format. No matter the task, if can you do it by repeating the same keystrokes or mouse clicks, you can create a macro to do it for you. By creating a macro, you can automate tasks which are time-consuming and require accuracy.

The Record Macro Dialog Box

The Record Macro dialog box is used to set record settings and record a new macro. You can specify the macro name and description, assign a button or keyboard shortcut to the macro, and specify whether the macro will be stored in the current document or the global template.

Macro Naming Rules

There are several rules to follow when you create macro names:

- The name must begin with a letter.
- The name must not contain spaces.
- The name can contain letters, numbers, and the underscore character.

Visual Basic for Applications (VBA)

Definition:

Visual Basic for Applications (VBA) is an event-driven programming language used to create macros in Microsoft Office applications. It can run code only from within a host application. When you record a macro, VBA automatically translates the keystrokes and commands into Visual Basic code language and stores the macro in code form.

> If you have a knowledge of VBA programming language and syntax, you can write code for macros directly in a VBA editor.

Example:

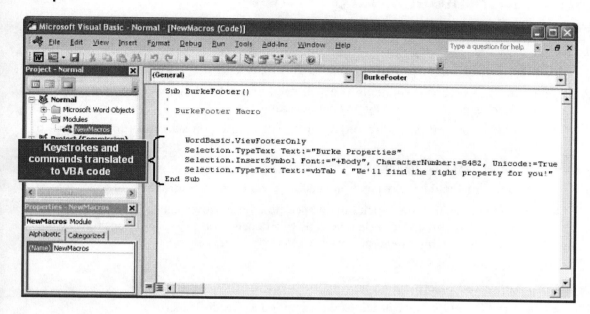

The Visual Basic Editor

You can use an add-in application called the Visual Basic Editor if you want to view or modify the VBA code for your macro. The Visual Basic Editor has its own three-part screen interface, menu bar, and Help system.

Visual Basic Editor Window Component	*Description*
Project Explorer	Lists the VBA modules in all open documents and templates.
	• The global template is listed as "Normal".
	• Open documents appear as "Project" objects.
	• Open templates appear as "TemplateProject" objects.
Properties window	Lists the properties of the item that is selected in the Project Explorer. A property is a characteristic of the item. For example, one property of a VBA module is the module's name.
Code window	Displays the VBA code for the selected project for editing.

VBA Modules

Each macro consists of a block of VBA code. Macro code is grouped together in larger VBA code blocks known as *modules*. Documents and templates can contain one or more modules, and modules can contain one or more macros.

Visual Basic

Visual Basic (VB) is a Microsoft programming language in which a programmer uses a graphical user interface to choose and modify preselected sections of code written in the BASIC programming language. It is used for creating self-contained Windows-based applications.

How to Create a Macro

Procedure Reference: Record a Macro

To record a macro:

1. Plan the sequence of steps and commands you want the macro to perform.

2. Determine any keyboard shortcuts you will need to substitute for specific mouse movements, such as clicking and dragging for selecting text.

3. Perform the steps you plan to record at least once before you start recording. This is to verify that:
   - The macro should produce the desired result.
   - The macro should not depend on specific content in the current document.
   - The macro should not depend upon specific mouse movements. For example, you cannot use the mouse to select text, as this depends on the specific position of the mouse. Use keyboard alternatives for selecting text.

4. Open a document.

5. Open the Record Macro dialog box.
   - On the Developer tab, in the Code group, click Record Macro.
   - On the Microsoft Office status bar, click the Record Macro button.
   - Or, on the View tab, in the Macros group, click the Macros drop-down button and select Record Macro.

6. Type a name for the macro in the Macro Name text box.

7. If necessary, assign a keyboard shortcut or a Quick Access toolbar button to the macro.

8. Select a location for the macro from the Store Macro In drop-down list.
   - Select the Normal template to make the macro available to all documents. This is the default.
   - Select the current document name to store the macro only in that document.

9. Type an optional description for the macro in the Description text box.

10. Click OK to start recording. The Stop Recording button appears on the status bar. The mouse pointer will appear with a small tape icon attached.

11. Perform the steps in the macro. As you record, you can click the Pause Recording/ Resume Recording button in the Code group or in the status bar to pause and resume recording.

12. Click Stop Recording in the Code or Macros group, or the Stop Recording button on the status bar.

13. If the macro is saved in a document, save the document using the .docm document type.

14. Run the macro to test it. If the macro is stored in the Normal template, test it in a new document.

ACTIVITY 10-2

Recording a Macro

Data Files:

Burke Footer.docm

Before You Begin

From C:\084894Data\Automating Tasks, open Burke Footer.docm

Scenario:

While Burke Properties has provided everyone with a macro to change the company name in all documents, you would also like to add a custom footer containing the company name to the documents that you create. It is time consuming to create this footer by hand in each document.

What You Do	How You Do It
1. You need to plan your macro. What are the general steps you must take to create the macro?	
2. Based on your plan, does this macro require you to record clicking and dragging mouse movements?	

3. **Create a new macro with the name, "BurkeFooter" and store it in the global template.**

   a. On the Ribbon, **select the Developer tab**.

   b. In the Code group, **click Record Macro**.

   c. In the Macro Name text box, **type *BurkeFooter***

   d. In the Store Macro In list box, **verify that All Documents (Normal.dotm) is selected** to make the macro available in all documents based on the global template.

   e. In the Description text box, **type *Creates standard document footer***

   f. **Click the Keyboard button** to display the Customize Keyboard dialog box.

   g. In the Press New Shortcut Key text box **press Alt** and **press *F***

   h. **Click Assign** to assign the keyboard shortcut to the macro.

   i. **Click Close** to begin the recording.

4. Record the macro to include the company name.

a. The mouse pointer now appears with a small tape icon attached. 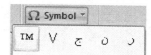 **Select the Insert tab.**

b. In the Header & Footer group, **click Footer.**

c. **Select Edit Footer.**

d. **Type** *Burke Properties*

e. On the Ribbon, **select the Insert tab.**

f. In the Symbols group, **click Symbol.**

g. **Select the trademark symbol.**

h. **Press Tab and type** *"We'll find the right property for you!"*

i. On the status bar, **click the Stop Recording button.**

j. **Save the document as** *My Burke Footer.docm* **and close it.**

5. Test the macro.

a. **Open a new blank document.**

b. **Press Alt+F** to run the BurkeFooter macro and insert the Burke Properties footer in the document.

6. Examine the macro code in the BurkeFooter macro.

a. On the Developer tab, in the Code group, **click Macros.**

b. **Verify that the BurkeFooter macro is first in the list and is selected by default. Click Edit** to open the macro for editing.

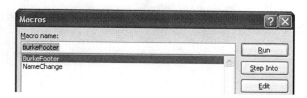

c. Observe the components of the macro code.

```
Sub BurkeFooter()
'
' BurkeFooter Macro
'
'
    WordBasic.ViewFooterOnly
    Selection.TypeText Text:="Burke Properties"
    Selection.InsertSymbol Font:="Times New Roman", CharacterNumber:=8482, _
        Unicode:=True
    Selection.TypeText Text:=vbTab & """We'll find the right property for you"
End Sub
```

d. **Choose File→Close And Return To Microsoft Word.**

e. **Close all the open documents without saving changes.**

Lesson 10 Follow-up

In this lesson, you learned how to use macros to automate common tasks. If you can run, record, and modify macros, you can use these powerful tools to automate any repetitive task that you perform, saving time and ensuring accuracy.

1. **In what ways have you seen macros used in your work environment?**

2. **Which repetitive tasks do you currently perform that you think you might automate with a macro?**

Follow-up

In this course, you created customized efficiency tools in Microsoft® Office Word 2007, and increased the complexity of your Microsoft Word 2007 documents by adding customized lists, tables, charts, and graphics. The skills you gained in this course will help you as you prepare for the Microsoft Certified Application Specialist exam for Microsoft Word 2007. These skills will also help you in your day-to-day work with Microsoft Word 2007, as you create more attractive and effective documents with less effort than before.

1. **Which feature of Word that you learned would help in accomplishing your day-to-day tasks more quickly and efficiently?**

2. **How does being able to customize your business documents help you in your work?**

What's Next?

Microsoft® Office Word 2007: Level 3 is the next course in this series. In that course, you will learn a variety of techniques for working with and collaborating on large documents and for using Microsoft Word 2007 to design and develop content for the World Wide Web.

Lesson Labs

Due to classroom setup constraints, some labs cannot be keyed in sequence immediately following their associated lesson. Your instructor will tell you whether your labs can be practiced immediately following the lesson or whether they require separate setup from the main lesson content.

Lesson 1 Lab 1

Modifying Lists

Activity Time: 15 minutes

Data Files:

Sales Lists.docx

Before You Begin:

Open the Sales Lists.docx file from the C:\084894Data\Managing Lists folder.

Scenario:

You're preparing a document for the monthly sales associates' meeting for Books And Beyond, a retail chain that combines a book and music store with an in-store coffee shop. There are two lists in the document: one lists CD sales by category and the other lists the top 10 customer book favorites. In the first list, you want to indicate how CD sales for the country music category relate to CD sales for the other music categories, and you realize that this relationship is hard to see with the list in its current order. You have almost completed the second list, when you realize that the list would look better with a different numbering style. You also want to add some commentary text after the ninth book entry.

---

1. In the Sales Lists document, **sort the Top Music Categories list in descending order by CD Sales.**

---

2. **Change the numbering style in the Top 10 Book Favorites list to 1) 2) 3) format.**

---

3. After the list item The President's Family, **add the comment paragraph,** *This book is appearing on the list for the first time this month!*

---

4. **Add the tenth list item as** *Dillon* **in the Title list and** *Jennifer Singles* **in the Author list.**

---

5. **Save the document as My Sales Lists.docx.**

Lesson 2 Lab 1

Customizing a Table and Chart

Activity Time: 15 minutes

Data Files:

Music Table.docx

Setup:

From the C:\084894Data\Customizing Tables and Charts folder, open Music Table.docx.

Scenario:

For the monthly sales associates' meeting of the company Books and Beyond, you are preparing a document containing a table that shows CD and tape sales for various categories. You've included the raw sales data and now you need to complete the table with a column showing sales totals for each category. You want to keep the sales people informed about the top categories based on total sales. You realize that the table columns are too large for their contents and think that the numeric data would look better if lined up to the left rather than to the right. Recently, there has been a heavy promotion of country music and therefore, you want to highlight this category in the table. The overall purpose of the table showing the top music categories may be revealed by the inclusion of an appropriate title. Your last step is to make it easier to portray the relationship between CD and tape sales in each category in a graphical way. You also want to show how each music category contributes to the overall sales of CDs and tapes.

1. In the music table document, **insert a Total Sales column to the right of the table.**

2. **Create formulas to show the total sales amounts for each category.**

3. **Sort the table in descending order by total sales.**

4. **Adjust the column widths to fit the table data.**

5. **Right-align the numbers in the last three columns of the table.**

6. **Create a new title row for the table containing the text,** *TOP MUSIC CATEGORIES* **centered across the other columns in the table.**

7. At the end of the document, **create a stacked-column chart from the data in the Category, CD Sales, and Tape Sales table columns.**

8. **Add a chart title that reads** *CD and Tape Sales Comparison*

9. **Delete the unnecessary legend marker.**

10. **Save the file as *My Music Table.docx***

Lesson 3 Lab 1

Creating Custom Styles

Activity Time: 15 minutes

Data Files:

BB Styles.docx

Setup:

Open the BB Styles.docx file from the C:\084894Data\Customizing Formatting folder.

Scenario:

You are preparing a marketing flyer to promote Books And Beyond's merchandise and services. You have laid out the text and formatting for the flyer. You would like the section headings in the flyer to be similar in style to the main heading but not quite as large. If you can create a look you like, you should identify a way to apply it easily to all the section headings in this document, and possibly in other new documents.

Your boss has also asked you to send her a short document with a list of Books And Beyond's special services, which include free delivery, "Meet the Author" Events, and rare book searches (both locally and using the Internet). You want this list to be highly presentable to attract the attention of the customers. You have an existing document with a well-formatted list in it, and you would like to be able to save that list format and apply it to your new list document.

1. In the BB Styles document, **format the "What Is Books And Beyond?" title to be centered, in small caps, and not italic.**

2. **Create a BB Heading paragraph style from the formatted text and add the style to the Normal template.**

3. **Apply the BB Heading style to the other three section titles in the document.**

4. **Create a new BB List style based on the list at the end of the document, and add the style to the Normal template.**

5. **Save the document as *My BB Styles.docx* and close the document.**

6. **In a new, blank document, type a heading that reads** *Our Special Services* **and press Enter to create a blank paragraph.**

7. **Format the "Our Special Services" heading text with the BB Heading style.**

8. **Apply the BB List style to the blank paragraph and enter the three main items for the bullet list.**

9. **Add sub-items for the two types of rare book searches.**

10. **Save the completed document as** *My Lab Styles.docx* **and close it.**

Lesson 4 Lab 1

Customizing a Picture

Activity Time: 15 minutes

Data Files:

Books Beyond Picture.docx

Setup:

Open the Books Beyond Picture.docx file from the C:\084894Data\Modifying Pictures folder.

Scenario:

You are working with a promotional document for Books And Beyond. You found a great piece of Clip Art on the Microsoft Office website and have inserted it into your document. However, its current placement disrupts the flow of the text too much—it would be better to set the picture off to the right side and let the text wrap around it. After you do this, you feel that the text looks a bit too ragged; and you can refine the look by adding some white space to the picture. Finally, you would like the picture to look lighter and more vivid, and so you think you might need to brighten it up.

1. In the Books Beyond Picture document, **set the layout properties for the picture to Square, and set the horizontal alignment to Middle Right.**

2. **Crop the picture to add white space to its left side and bottom.**

3. **Change the Brightness setting for the picture to 60%.**

4. Save the document as *My Books Beyond Picture.docx*.

Lesson 5 Lab 1

Customizing Graphics

Activity Time: 15 minutes

Data Files:

BB Graphics.doc

Before You Begin

Open the BB Graphics.docx file from the C:\084894Data\Creating Customized Graphics Elements folder.

Scenario:

You are working on a promotional document for Books And Beyond. You have the text entered in the document and now you want to add visual interest to it. You can identify at least three places where some graphic elements could enhance the document. One is to create a more decorative overall title for the document. The next is to highlight the subtitle "What Is Books & Beyond?" by adding a graphic background. The third is to create a diagram that displays the main idea of the text—that the Books & Beyond experience builds on its foundation as a respected bookseller by adding best-selling music and a popular coffee bar.

1. In the BB Graphics document, **replace the Books & Beyond title with a piece of WordArt that reads Books & Beyond.**

2. Around the "What Is Books & Beyond?" text, **draw a shape of your choice and fill the shape with a color of your choice.**

3. Set the layout properties for the shape to Behind Text.

4. Insert a basic pyramid SmartArt graphic at the beginning of the "Some people say" paragraph.

5. Insert the text elements for the three components of the pyramid diagram: *Books, Music,* and *Coffee* from top to bottom, respectively.

6. Set the size of the SmartArt graphic to approximately a 3-inch square.

7. Set the text wrapping for the SmartArt graphic to Square.

8. **Align the SmartArt graphic to the right.**

9. **Format the text in each shape of the SmartArt graphic so that the font size increases with the size of each shape in the graphic.**

10. **Save the completed document as *My BB Graphics.docx* and close it.**

Lesson 6 Lab 1

Inserting Content Using Quick Parts

Activity Time: 15 minutes

Data Files:

Burke Reports.docx

Setup:

Open the Burke Reports.docx file from the C:\084894Data\Inserting Content Using Quick Parts folder.

Scenario:

Burke Properties has decided to define certain standards for all the documents prepared in the company. According to these standards, all documents need to have any special status clearly marked, be numbered, show the date, and include a standard postscript and the name of the file.

1. **Save the postscript paragraph of the document as a building block in a custom category named Signatures.**

2. **Insert an Urgent watermark building block.**

3. After the address block at the top of the document, **insert a Date field.**

4. **Insert the FileName field into the footer.**

5. **Save the document as *My Burke Reports.docx***

6. **Update the FileName field in the footer.**

7. **Save and close the document.**

Lesson 7 Lab 1

Controlling Text Flow

Activity Time: 15 minutes

Data Files:

Books Beyond News.docx

Before You Begin:

From C:\084894Data\Controlling Text Flow, open Books Beyond News.docx.

Scenario:

Your supervisor has handed you text for the first issue of the new Books & Beyond newsletter and has asked you to format the text flow in the newsletter appropriately. Most newsletters you've seen use a two-column format, and you think this will be suitable for this information. However, there are two areas of the document that will not work well in columns because they are too wide: the masthead section at the beginning of the document and the tables at the end of the document that list current best sellers.

1. In the Books & Beyond News document, **insert a continuous section break at the beginning of the "Have you ever" paragraph.**

2. **Insert a Next Page section break at the beginning of the "Best Sellers Lists" heading at the bottom of the first page.**

3. **Format Section 2 into two equal columns with a line in between.**

4. **Create two columns from a point just before the "Non-fiction best sellers" table forward through the rest of the document.**

5. **Insert a column break just before the "Fiction bestsellers" table.**

6. **Preview the document.**

7. **Save the document as *My Books Beyond News.docx*.**

Lesson 8 Lab 1

Using Templates to Automate Document Creation

Activity Time: 15 minutes

Conditions:

You have an active connection to the Internet.

Scenario:

You have to prepare an agenda for a weekly company meeting. You realize that most of the agenda information is the same from week to week, with the only change being the date, location, and occasionally an additional agenda item or two. You decide to create an agenda template so that you can reuse the basic format for future meetings.

1. Use the Informal Meeting Agenda template from Microsoft Office online to create an agenda document containing reusable information of your choice.

2. Save the agenda document in the Automating Document Creation folder as *My Burke Agenda.dotx* and update the file format to Word 2007.

3. Test the My Burke Agenda template by creating a new agenda document based on it.

4. Save the new document as *My Burke Agenda Test.docx* and close the document.

Lesson 9 Lab 1

Performing Mail Merges

Activity Time: 15 minutes

Data Files:

BB Form Letter.docx

Before You Begin:

You have a print driver installed and configured as your default printer.

Scenario:

The Books & Beyond store manager has asked you to send out a welcome letter to two new customers who have just joined the Books & Beyond Reading Rewards sales incentive program. The letter is stored on the computer, but your manager has given you the new customers' names written on a piece of paper. You need to create and print letters with each customer's name and address, and print envelopes to go along with the letters. The manager has asked you to provide her with a hard copy of the letters to sign and an electronic copy for her files. You would like to automate the task of generating personalized letters for each customer instead of repeating the process of creating each one manually.

1. In a new, blank Word document, using data of your choice, **create a table containing the first names, last names, street addresses, city names, states, and ZIP Codes of two customers to be used as a data source.**

2. **Save the data source document as** *My BB Data Source.docx* **and close the document.**

3. In a blank document, **use the Mail Merge wizard pane to select BB Form Letter as the main document, My BB Data Source as the data source, and to insert the address block and greeting line fields.**

4. **Complete the merge and print the output.**

5. **Save the merge output document as** *My BB Merge.docx* **and close any open documents.**

6. **Use the Mail Merge wizard pane to create an envelope document, select My BB Data Source as the data source, and insert an address block field in the envelope.**

7. **Print the merged envelopes.**

8. **Close the envelope document without saving changes.**

Lesson 10 Lab 1
Automating a Task

Activity Time: 15 minutes

Data Files:

BB Macro.docx, BB Macro Test.docx

Scenario:

Books & Beyond has recently revised its corporate communications standards. Previously, it was acceptable to refer to the company as either "Books And Beyond" or "Books & Beyond". Now, the company wants the name to appear consistently as "Books & Beyond". You would like to find a quick and easy way to perform this task in all your documents.

1. In the BB Macro document, **create a new macro named BBname and store it in the Normal template.**

2. **Record the macro as you search for and replace all instances of "Books And Beyond" with the text "Books & Beyond".**

3. **Stop recording the macro.**

4. **Save the document as** *My BB Macro.docx* **and close it.**

5. In the BB Macro Test document, **run the BBname macro to test it.**

6. **Save the document as** *My BB Macro Test.docm*

7. **Preview the document.**

8. **Close the document.**

Solutions

Activity 10-2

1. **You need to plan your macro. What are the general steps you must take to create the macro?**

   Create and name the macro; on the Insert tab, in the Header & Footer group click Footer and select Edit Footer; type the footer information.

2. **Based on your plan, does this macro require you to record clicking and dragging mouse movements?**

   No, it does not.

Glossary

argument
The set of values on which a function operates.

building block
A preformatted piece of content that can be reused within or across Word documents.

cell alignment
A text-positioning option that enables you to control the placement of text within a cell.

cell merge
A method of altering the configuration of groups of cells in a table.

cell split
A method of dividing a single cell into a group of adjacent cells.

character spacing
A specialized formatting technique that controls the size of characters and the distance between them.

character style
A style that includes only character formatting.

chart
A visual representation of the relationships between one or more series of numbers in table.

compression
a method of reducing the file size by using fewer bits to store the same amount of information.

cropping
An image-editing technique that helps remove portions of the picture and reduces image size to reshape the picture as you desire.

custom style
A style that has formatting characteristics defined by a user.

data source
A collection of information that forms the input for the merge.

delimited text file
A plain text file in which fields and rows are separated by tabs, commas, or a tilde (~).

document template
A template used to create a specific type of document.

document themes
Sets of formatting options that can be applied to the entire document to ensure a consistent look.

drawing canvas
A container for other graphics that enables you to manipulate shapes as a group.

Drop Cap

A text effect feature in Word that creates a large capital letter at the beginning of a paragraph.

equation

In Word, a specialized document element that can contain complex mathematical symbols and perform customized calculations.

field codes

The programming instructions that determine the value of a field.

field

An instruction code inserted into a Word document that dynamically displays specific pieces of variable information, such as the current date, time, or page number.

forms

Word templates that include special content controls to simplify data entry in the template.

formula

A mathematical expression that can be used to perform calculations on data in a table.

function

A predefined expression that takes on values and performs an operation.

global template

A template that stores settings that are available to all open documents.

kerning

A publishing technique that expands or condenses individual pairs of letters to create the appearance of even spacing.

linked style

A style that can contain paragraph formatting but that can be applied to selected text within a paragraph.

linked text boxes

One or more text boxes connected so that text flows from the first to subsequent boxes.

list style

A style that contains list-specific formatting options.

macro

A task automation tool that executes a set of commands to automate frequently repeated steps.

mail merge

A word processor feature that produces multiple documents from a template and a single source of data.

main merge document

In a mail merge, the document that contains the fixed data and placeholder fields for the variable data.

merge field

A placeholder for variable content in a main merge document.

multilevel list

A list with items on multiple levels where the number or bullet format is different for the different levels.

orphan line

A single line of a multiline paragraph that appears by itself at the bottom of a page or column.

paragraph style

A style that has formatting characteristics of characters and paragraphs and which is applied to a paragraph as a whole.

picture brightness

An image-control setting that changes the amount of white present in the colors or shades of gray in a graphic element. Brightness is set as a percentage.

picture contrast

An image-control setting that controls the amount of difference between adjacent colors or shades of gray in a graphic element.

pixel

An individual dot of color on a computer screen.

point

A publishing measurement, equivalent to 1/72 of an inch, used to measure font sizes or spacing.

pull quotes

A predefined text box that serves as a placeholder for important information within a document.

section break

A feature that marks the boundaries between multiple sections in a document.

shape

A predefined figure that you can insert into a Word document to complement the text within it.

sidebar

A predefined text box that usually functions as a standalone supplement to the main text, often aligned with one edge of the page.

SmartArt graphic

A preset image used to illustrate information in a document.

sort field

An individual item separated by a field separator character that you use as a basis for sorting lists or a table column.

template wizard

A tool from previous versions of Word that uses a multi-page format to guide users through the process of creating standard documents.

template

A predefined Word document with a .dotx file extension that is used as a basis for creating other new documents.

text box

A graphic entity that serves as a container for text or graphics.

text columns

A layout that organizes and presents text as columns on a page.

text direction

A text-positioning option that enables you to change the direction of the text flow.

text wrapping style

A text formatting style that determines how adjacent text will appear along with a graphic.

Visual Basic for Applications (VBA)

An event-driven programming language used to create macros in Microsoft Office applications.

widow line

A single line of a multiline paragraph that appears by itself at the top of a page or column.

WordArt objects

Decorative text elements you insert as graphic objects in a document.

Index

formula, 31
formula entries
  default, 34
function, 32

G
Global templates
  See: template types

H
HTML, 173

I
Insert Merge Fields
  See: Write & Insert Fields group
Insert Merge Fields dialog box, 176
Insert tab, 102

K
kerning, 47

L
Label Options dialog box, 185
Line And Page Breaks tab, 136
  Also See: paragraph flow
list appearance
  customization options, 12
list style, 11

M
macro, 198
  naming rules, 204
  new, 204
  security, 199
macro security system, 199
MacroButton field, 163
  syntax, 163
Macros dialog box, 199
mail merge, 170
  resuming, 175
mail merge process, 174, 175, 174
  Also See: Mailings tab
Mail Merge Recipients dialog box, 176
Mail Merge task pane, 175
Mail Merge Wizard, 176
Mailings tab, 174, 175
main merge document
  saving original, 175

merge field, 171
merge fields
  types, 171
merge options
  for envelopes, 185
  for labels, 185
Microsoft Office FoxPro, 173
Microsoft Office Query, 173
Microsoft Office Word dialog box, 175
modify a style
  in other documents, 51
Modify Building Block dialog box, 125
modules, 205
  Also See: VBA modules
multilevel list, 11
Multilevel List button, 12
Multilevel List gallery, 56
multilevel lists, 11

N
Normal template, 49
  Also See: template types
numbered list
  convert to multilevel list, 11
Numbering button, 8

O
orphan line, 136

P
paragraph flow, 136
paragraph style, 46
picture brightness, 75
picture contrast, 74
picture positioning options, 82
point, 47
PRODUCT, 32
pull quote, 89

Q
Quick Parts, 116
Quick Parts menu, 116

R
Recolor gallery, 76
  Also See: Adjust group
Record Macro dialog box, 204
renumbering options, 8

Looking for media files?

They are now conveniently located at www.elementk.com/courseware-file-downloads

Downloading is quick and easy:

1. Visit www.elementk.com/courseware-file-downloads
2. In the search field, type in either the part number or the title
3. Of the courseware titles displayed, choose your title by clicking on the name
4. Links to the data files are located in the middle of the screen
5. Follow the instructions on the screen based upon your web browser

Note that there may be other files available for download in addition to the course files.

Approximate download times:

The amount of time it takes to download your data files will vary according to the file's size and your Internet connection speed. A broadband connection is highly recommended. The average time to download a 10 mb file on a broadband connection is less than 1 minute.